ROUND THE WORLD
WITH FAMOUS AUTHORS

Round the World

WITH

Famous Authors

with an Introduction by
LOWELL THOMAS

Published in cooperation with
PAN AMERICAN WORLD AIRWAYS, INC.
by
DOUBLEDAY & COMPANY, INC.
Garden City, New York

The photographs on the preceding pages are: Trancura River in Chile; the White Pagoda overlooking the harbor of Hong Kong; the village pond in Singleton, Sussex, England; the Cathedral of Notre Dame towering majestically above the river Seine and the bookstalls on the Left Bank; England's stately Houses of Parliament on the Thames; Neuschwanstein Castle in Bavaria with Lake Alpsee in the background; Hamilton harbor, Bermuda; strange and beautiful Monument Valley in Arizona and Utah; and Hawaii's beautiful Waikiki beach with Diamond Head.

Library of Congress Catalog Card Number 58–10855

Copyright, 1958, by Doubleday & Company, Inc.

All Rights Reserved

Printed in the United States of America

BROWN & BIGELOW, ST. PAUL, MINN., U.S.A.

Contents

Color Photographs

Introduction
by Lowell Thomas

An interesting study could be made of the format of travel books. Myriads of them have been published for some twenty-five hundred years, and most have consisted, of course, of somebody telling how he went to this place or that, usually describing a more or less consecutive journey. But there have been other patterns, too. Take the case of the first great travel writer of them all.

In a formal sense, Herodotus does not relate the tale of journeys afar in his memorable book, "History of the Persian Wars." The travel part of it is only incidental—or so it would seem in the formal pattern of the masterpiece. Nevertheless, if Herodotus was the Father of History, he was also the Father of Travel Books. In his masterpiece, his accounts of the journeys he made and what he saw and heard are about as important as his account of marches and battles in the conflict between Greece and Persia. Many would consider the travel part the more beguiling.

Herodotus loved to tell stories of strange places. In his travels in the world of the eastern Mediterranean, he gathered marvelous yarns—some of them among the most magnificent whoppers in all literature. So we can forgive Voltaire for saying: "Father of History—Father of Lies." However, we may note that the old Greek, when telling a tall one, with relish, will carefully say —he was told this in Egypt, or Persia, or whatever. For example, his explanation of the source of the Nile—the river rising from a huge underground fountain, far to the south of Egypt—he says he got from an Egyptian priest at Sais.

Of particular interest is the way Herodotus wove his travel tales into his historical account of the Persian Wars. The army of the King of Kings is marching, with detachments from many nations, all the way from India to the Caspian. So the historian names them in geographical order, giving an account of the country from which each body of soldiers—the Indians, the Scythians, for example—comes. This is one way in which he weaves travel material into the sequences of history, and also includes accounts of his own journeys. The format is ingenious—virtually a travel book incorporated in a history of memorable events.

But now let's look at the most famous travel book of all, the best known account of marvelous journeying in exotic places, which had a great effect on subsequent exploration. The book of Marco Polo has comparatively little account of travel. The Venetian who made his way, with his father and uncle, to the court of Kubla Khan, gives only a sketchy account of the astonishing itinerary by which he got there. This, in fact, is disappointing, but Marco Polo's format is not one of telling a personal story. Most of his book consists of descriptions of countries and cities, a veritable catalogue of these—the inference being that he visited these places, and tells of what he saw. But that is largely by implication, Marco Polo's format doesn't concern itself with the details of how he contrived to get from one place to another in such far flung regions.

One might also note the most successful of all travel novels, "Around The World In Eighty Days," and the way it was written by that remarkable non-traveler, Jules Verne. His travels and imagination took him far under the sea and to the moon in other books, not to mention the mere circumnavigation of the world. Jules Verne did his traveling in the library, the Bibliothèque in Paris, and from books he got his accounts of strange places for Phineas Fogg's trip around the world.

So now we have another format for a travel book—a circumnavigation of the world through the eyes of famous writers and illustrated with colorful pictures. Something new in travel books—and a welcome innovation.

NORTHERN EUROPE

On the following double-page spread is a photograph of the 8th-century Abbey of Mont-Saint-Michel, France, which is connected with the mainland by a mile-long causeway.

Mont-Saint-Michel

The church stands high on the summit of this granite rock, and on its west front is the platform, to which the tourist ought first to climb. From the edge of this platform, the eye plunges down, two hundred and thirty-five feet, to the wide sands or the wider ocean, as the tides recede or advance, under an infinite sky, over a restless sea, which even we tourists can understand and feel without books or guides; but when we turn from the western view, and look at the church door, thirty or forty yards from the parapet where we stand, one needs to be eight centuries old to know what this encrusted mass of encrusted architecture meant to its builders, and even then one must still learn to feel it. The man who wanders into the twelfth century is lost, unless he can grow prematurely young.

Montparnasse

The events of my life have led me at one time and another to dwell transitorily in pretty well all the worlds of Paris, even in the closed world of the Boulevard St. Germain; but that which I like best, better than the discreet circle that has its center in what is now called the Avenue Foch, better than the cosmopolitan crew that patronized Larue's and the Café de Paris, better than the noisy sordid gaiety of Montmartre is that section of which the artery is the Boulevard du Montparnasse. In my youth I spent a year in a tiny apartment near the Lion de Belfort, on the fifth floor, from which I had a spacious view of the cemetery. Montparnasse has still for me the tranquil air of a provincial town that was characteristic of it then. When I pass through the dingy narrow Rue d'Odessa I remember with a pain the shabby restaurant where we used to foregather to dine, painters and illustrators and sculptors, I, but for Arnold Bennett on occasion, the only writer, and sit late discussing excitedly, absurdly, angrily painting and literature. It is still a pleasure to me to stroll down the boulevard and look at the young people who are as young as I was then and invent stories for myself about them. When I have nothing better to do I take a taxi and go and sit in the old Café du Dôme. It is no longer what it was then, the meeting place exclusively of Bohemia; the small tradesmen of the neighborhood have taken to visiting it, and strangers from the other side of the Seine come to it in the hope of seeing a world that has ceased to exist. Students come to it still, of course, painters and writers, but most of them are foreigners; and when you sit there you hear around you as much Russian, Spanish, German and English as French. But I have a notion that they are saying very much the same sort of things as we said forty years ago, only they speak of Picasso instead of Manet and of André Breton instead of Guillaume Appollinaire. My heart goes out to them.

The Eiffel Tower

From *Paris! Paris!* by Irwin Shaw, in *Holiday,* copyright, 1953, by The Curtis Publishing Co., reprinted by permission of the author.

First, there should be a general, bird's-eye view of the city, and the best place for that is the top of the Eiffel Tower. From there, the city lies embraced by its winding river and flows in a silvery haze over its moderate hills and its central plain. You can look out over the homes and the shops and the cemeteries and places of worship of three million people and you can see the hill in Montmartre where the Temple of Mercury used to stand and where St. Denis was beheaded. You can trace the course of the river and see where the canals join it and the Marne, and you can tell your girl about the Norsemen who sailed up the river in their oared galleys in the ninth century, jovially axing the farmers and the city dwellers along the banks, as was the custom of travelers at that time.

Paris in the Fall

From *Paris,* by Francis Steegmuller, copyright ©, 1957, by Saturday Review, Inc., reprinted by permission of the publisher.

Paris becomes itself in October. . . . The new plays open, and Parisians make up their own minds about them. The excellent newspaper *Le Monde* publishes some of the most intelligent criticism being written about the theatre today—the dramatic reviews by Robert Kemp. But Kemp and his colleagues don't make or break plays like their New York opposites. . . . The function of the Parisian review is to stimulate. This is the time of year when discreet little *entrefilets* in the newspapers announce, without fanfare, the opening of new restaurants that may prove to be superb. It's fun to try them, to speculate whether they'll last. The mortality rate is high. If the ones new to Paris are disappointing, there's always an old one to try that's new to you, or one of your favorites to revisit. . . . The weather? "C'est la saison," as the Parisians say, which means that the weather is "seasonable." Don't expect the bright, crisp weather of our Indian summer. Paris is damper and greyer, though throughout the winter come mild and golden days. As the days grow shorter dusk can fall on an overcast Paris by four o'clock, and it's cozy to have the valet de chambre light the charcoal briquets in the fireplace of your hotel room, and sit there having your tea in the cheerful glow, watching the violet twilight creep over the city without.

Autumn is the season for a visit to Versailles, with the gold and russet leaves falling nostalgically in the allées, evoking generations of history and grandeur; and it is the season too for an excursion to the chateaux of the Loire, especially to Chenonceaux with its parterres full of fall flowers, and to Burgundy where the wine is best with pheasant and partridge. . . . After a snowfall the Tuileries Gardens are an unforgettable sight; and the snowcaps on the statue of the Vert Galant and his horse on the Pont Neuf bring to life the most haunting cityscapes of Pissaro. . . .

Paris in the Spring

From *Sutton's Places,* copyright, 1954, by Horace Sutton, reprinted by permission of Henry Holt and Company, Inc.

It happened by the merest chance that spring and I arrived together in Paris this year, and we were equally glad to be there. I had come in the night from across the Channel, where an ordinary spring was biting through the topcoats of Americans and reaching their bones, leaving the English in their suits and bowlers, topcoats in their closets, not a whit disturbed beyond their catarrh, which is expected, accepted, and seasonal. Somewhere in the dark night, I had to get up and swing open the full French windows to let the mildness in. You could put your bare foot on the stone of the tiny terrace outside the window without its growing cold, and you could look up at the Vendôme with the moon coming down on Napoleon's head on top of the column. No one stirred the checkerboard of lights and darkness along the Rue Castiglione, and the moon was wasting itself on the gold-tipped spikes of the Tuileries.

By morning the spring warmth was sending waves up from the pavement, and, like an old dancer, Paris responded to the familiar music with the old routine. The tables grew like sudden moss on the rocks of the pavements outside the cafes. The lovers embraced in noonday passion on a bench in the Louvre quadrangle. And also under an arch at the Rue de Rivoli, and in a narrow alley in Montmartre. . . .

Cathedral of Notre-Dame

From *Notre-Dame of Paris,* copyright, 1952, 1955, by Allan Temko, reprinted by permission of The Viking Press, Inc.

There are as many ways to approach Notre-Dame as there are streets in Paris or roads in France. But perhaps the best is along the quays of the Left Bank on a summer morning, following the river, catching glimpses of the Cathedral through the trees. From a distance the great double towers alone are visible, guarding Paris with their brotherly strength. The strength was expected, but what was unforseen was their pure white radiance. The towers are a startling white in the vivid Parisian air. They are as new, as bold, as young and optimistic as seven hundred years ago, when the last stones were fitted in the cornices before the year 1250. Quite suddenly the towers vanish in the green chestnuts and oaks, and the charming stage scenery of Paris intervenes, like a blithe Dufy. Paris, the world's Paris: the crowded bookstalls, the intellectual posture of the promeneurs; the barges smacking up-river, the Louvre across the Pont de Arts, the elegant triangle of the island in the Seine, the Pont Neuf, the roofs of the Cité; and again the white towers of Notre-Dame, perhaps with tricolors flying, and the blue sky of France as a background. Finally, at the Place Saint-Michel, the entire western façade of the Cathedral comes into sight, like an enormous postcard, and so familiar that the tourist puts down his Kodak at once.

Cathedral at Strasbourg

From *The Rhine,* copyright ©, 1955, by Felizia Seyd, reprinted by permission of Doubleday & Company, Inc.

The Rue des Grandes Arcades on your right . . . takes you in the direction of the cathedral across the small lively Gutenberg Square, with a fine statue of the inventor of printing by David d'Angers. The approach to the cathedral is confusing, however, as the church does not come into view until you are practically at its steps. Then, as the vast western façade looms up of a sudden, your heart leaps and the world is no longer sad.

Before you is a three-dimensional world in rose-colored stone. Vault rises above vault, their vertical lines broken by three galleries. Mighty butresses taper up from story to story. Turrets, archways, miniature columns, and perforated roses alternate with statues of angels and saints, men, beasts and symbolical figures, all of them part of a perfectly integrated design and dominated and held together by the "Sun of Justice," symbolized by the giant rose window in the center catching the light of the setting sun. Gradually, as the eye travels upward from story to story, it reaches the solitary tower culminating in the spire. And the spire leaves you breathless. It is a living thing, a cry of joy rising to pierce the clouds, a song, a gesture of defiance, proclaiming man's everlasting triumph over death, misery, and pain. "I have seen Chartres and Antwerp," said Victor Hugo. "I needed Strasbourg."

Chartres

From *Pigs in Clover,* copyright, 1931, by Frances Noyes Hart, reprinted by permission of Brandt & Brandt.

There is no bonnier town in France than Chartres, to my mind. Across the narrow flow of its river Eure, little bridges are flung lavishly, and women kneel beside its waters, bare-armed and bare-headed in their faded rose and lilac dresses, pounding out clothes at its friendly edge. Their laughter reached us as we crossed, and we leaned far out of the car windows so that we could see the gardens spilling over into it, and the little houses—dove colored, fawn colored, mouse colored—thrusting so eagerly to get closer to it that they almost fell in. Across the bridge a street wound, narrow and carefree as a country lane, and we knew that if we followed it we would find the world's treasure at the end. And we followed—and we found it.

Chartres Cathedral is a golden gray, so soft that you want to stretch out your hand and stroke it, and some miracle has tempered its austere magnificence with so much grace and hallowed friendliness that it blessed us simply to stand quiet, and look at it. There in his appointed niche the tall young angel was still standing, holding the great sundial before him like a shield; but as we looked we saw that he was smiling a little, grave and beautiful, and holding it toward us so that we could share his secret. That evening we wanted only to see the angel gilded by the dying sun; the glory within the walls was for the morning.

15

Quimper the Provincial

From *Enchanted Brittany,* by Amy Oakley, copyright, 1930, by The Century Co., reprinted by permission of the publisher, Appleton-Century-Crofts, Inc.

Situated on the picturesque quay of the Odet within a few minutes' walk from the Hôtel de l'Epée are the potteries of Locmaria. Here for centuries two rather primitive establishments have turned out the hand-painted *faïence* to be seen everywhere in Brittany. Not only in Paris but even in the United States lovers of artistic ware cherish plates and platters, cups and saucers, bowls and jugs, decorated with the delightful figure of a Breton peasant in gala attire.

The establishment Henriot nestles at the foot of the linden-clad slope of Mont-Frugy. We were greeted on the day of our visit by an impeccable "buttons," with ears as protuberant as the handles of a Quimper jug. He led us past wood neatly stacked for use in the ovens and up steep steps. We found ourselves in the midst of the primitive yet flourishing industry. The only machine in use was the foot-wheel of certain potters. We watched a dour fellow in sabots fashioning a lump of clay. He clapped it on his wheel, it whirled, water moistened it, the man clipped the edges and, presto! a perfectly mouled plate. Nearby pitchers were in construction, passed fresh from the wheel to a girl who tweaked out lips with the knowing turn of an implement. Other girls made handles skilfully. Buttons informed us that "the artists are the best paid, especially those who do the décor riche."

French Food

From *Understanding the French,* copyright, 1954, 1955, by Elliot Paul, reprinted by permission of Random House, Inc.

Too much stress has been laid by writers, by and large, on the fancy eating that tourists and rich Frenchmen do in Paris, and the famous restaurants of Dijon, Lyons, Toulouse, Marseilles and Rouen. The significance of food in France is the fact that the French, generally, are well nourished and at a surprisingly low cost.

In the regions devoted to agriculture—that is to say, nearly all of the country—the peasants enjoy a varied, balanced diet, well flavored with aromatics, pungents, condiments, spices and wine. Farm women have passed on their skill and knowledge through generations that span twenty centuries and nearly every kind of governmental evolution or experiment. The inexpensive cuts of meat have been composed into traditional dishes—stews, soups, scallops, rice dishes, sausages, creams and grills. The best of the French sauces are enjoyed in peasant houses. In Paris and the other cities, the white-collar class and the small proprietors do as well as the peasants, and enjoy even more variety, so well are the city markets organized.

Morning in Cannes

From *A Room in Paris*, by Peggy Mann, copyright, 1955, by Peggy Mann Houlton, reprinted by permission of Doubleday & Company, Inc.

They drove slowly down the broad Croisette. Janet dropped the stole from her shoulders and stretched her arms out along the sun-warmed leather seat of the Hotchkiss convertible.

To the left the white hotels of Cannes slid past in slow and elegant procession, waiting for the evening hours, when the city was theirs and the colored lights played into the palm trees, and the ballrooms and bars came alive with laughter and champagne and Latin-American rhythms.

But the luxury had moved outside now, into the sunshine. The terrace of the Carlton was crowded as guests sipped apéritifs, read the papers, traded gossip made the night before. The fashionable morning stroll had started along the Croisette—a bright blond woman in a barebacked sun dress leading her proud black poodle—a stiff, starched Nanny grasping a neat little boy by the hand—a paunchy gentleman in dark glasses and flowered sports shirt who stopped to sniff the blossoms on a mimosa tree.

On the following double-page spread is a photograph of Bruges, Belgium, with the old world charm of its time-mellowed buildings. More than 50 bridges span the canals.

Bruges

From *Belgium and Lux-emburg,* edited by Doré Ogrizek, copyright, 1950, by the McGraw-Hill Book Company, Inc., reprinted by permission.

Bruges . . . has a beauty which captivates us at the first glance and which is always new without ever becoming exhausted. However long we stay in Bruges, whether it be a few hours, just sufficient time to take the usual boat trip from the Quai du Miroir to the Lac d'Amour, or whether it be for a few days, a few weeks, wandering in the most out-of-the-way streets, searching for the small statue, the old gateway, the old rustic corner not mentioned in the guide-books, we leave Bruges with a feeling of bewildered contentment.

Bruges has kept its 13th century boundaries, its old gateways, one of which, the Ghent Gate, opens onto land. The other, the Ostend Gate, opens towards the sea. Both these gateways, with their grey towers, are reflected in the water of the canal. As in days gone by, life in Bruges is concentrated on the Grand Place, at the foot of the belfry, which has lost its spire and still leans towards the southwest. The brick walls of the façade, slightly yellow, have rusty hues which were Victor Hugo's delight. A provincial hotel, a post office in Gothic style take the place of the Winterhalle. Opposite is the old Cranenburg cabaret, where Maximilian was prisoner for four months, and the ancient Bouchoute house, with its large dial which indicates the direction of the wind. Close by is the Place du Bourg more ostentatious and dignified. The oldest town hall in Belgium and the former office of the clerks of the Criminal Court occupy the farther end of it. This town hall has forty-eight statues of the Flanders's nobles since Baldwin the Iron Arm.

The Wonderful House of Erasmus

From *All the Best in Belgium and Luxembourg,* © 1956, by Sydney Clark, reprinted by permission of Dodd, Mead & Company.

In Brussels' suburb of Anderlecht there is a charming old house of the Gothic period where Desiderius Erasmus lived for a part of the year 1521. It was actually the property of a religious order but so great is the fame of the Dutch humanist that, although he was only a short-time tenant, it is always called the Erasmus House. . . .

The house is outstandingly charming in itself and to put us in the right medieval mood the guardian sets in motion a concealed record player which fills the mansion with lovely old Gregorian choral music enriched by choral accompaniment. Several of the rooms are now used as a museum of folklore and, more importantly, of Erasmus relics, the room that is devoted to his literary works being a particularly pleasing one, its walls covered with gilded sheep leather. His most celebrated book, *In Praise of Folly,* is seen in Latin, French, English and other languages, the original Latin title being *Moriae Encomium.* A first edition in Latin, bearing the date 1511, is on display. In the beautiful garden of this house an exhibition of some forty or fifty modern sculptures is held in *even* years, all summer. . . .

Belgium—A Kitchen Garden

From *Belgium,* by William Davenport, copyright ©, 1958, by Nelson Double-day, Inc., reprinted by permission of the publisher.

An English visitor once described Belgium as a vast kitchen garden, and it is true that, despite the predominance of industry, Belgian farmers are among the world's best. More than sixty per cent of the country is under intensive and skillful cultivation. The agricultural yield per acre is one of the highest in the world, and farming supplies seventy per cent of the nation's own food needs. The chief crops are oats, wheat, rye, barley, sugar beets, potatoes, and vegetables. Another major item is flax, basis for the linen industry. Farm holdings in general are small, the result of family subdivisions throughout the ages. In Flanders, the factory worker frequently cultivates his own small holding, doubling as a farmer after a hard day's work at the mill. Kitchen gardens are to be seen everywhere, but there is increasing mechanization of farm work.

Modern technical methods of extraction have increased Belgium's yield of sugar from sugar beets by forty-five per cent in recent years, and sugar is now a major national product. Delicious Belgian chocolates, preserves, biscuits, and *pains d'épice* or spice bread, a popular Belgian specialty, are a few of the products stemming from the sugar industry.

Brussels

From *The Land and People of Belgium,* by Dorothy Loder, copyright ©, 1957, by Dorothy Loder, published by J. B. Lippincott Company, reprinted by permission.

Brussels is sometimes called a "little Paris," but it approaches the French capital's exciting beauty only in the splendor of the Grand' Place with its town hall and guild houses, in the lines of Saint Gudule against the horizon or the bulk of the Justice Building looming on the height above old Brussels. . . .

In the beginning, Brussels was a water city like Liège, Ghent or Bruges. The Grand' Place is said to occupy the site of an ancient marsh. Traffic careens through streets where canals once bore barges. . . . Although lacking great beauty, *la Capitale* possesses its own charm. For example, you never tire of the skyline. The tower of the town hall, delicate as the spun-sugar topping to a wedding cake, especially when the Grand' Place is illuminated at night, dominates a welter of dark, Spanish-tiled roofs, domes, slender belfries and jutting gables, with a few television antennas sprouting among the stone or gilded metal stars, birds, animals, ships and statues which decorate the gables. Then there are the chimney pots! Who can forget them, smoking into the low clouds on a gray morning, four or five to the chimney, each pot leading to the flue of a coal stove set up in some apartment or room? Only a few expensive new building supply their tenants with central heat. Sometimes you chance on delightful byways just out of the wash of crowds and traffic: pale, graceful houses dozing about an ancient church or encircling a monument set in a grassy plot, old palaces seen through an archway down a cobbled street, a blind alley beginning with a wrought-iron gate and ending in a tree that branches toward the shabby houses on each side; a ruined tower, last remnant of the city's early fortifications.

21

The Homey Outlook

From *Snapshots of the Dutch,* by George Mikes, in *Benelux 1958,* Edited by Eugene Fodor, published by David McKay Company Inc., reprinted by permission.

To me—and many others—the main charm of Holland is to be found in the streets. There is no other country in the world—except Italy and the Flemish part of Belgium—where such long rows of artistic and charming houses delight the eye. But the architectural beauty of the houses is only one side of the general delightful impression. The spirit of the streets is the other. . . .

The English segregate their houses from the street as much as they can; the Dutch, on the other hand, link their houses with the streets. The Englishman's main concern is that no one should be able to look into his home from the street; the Dutchman's main concern is that he should be able to see from his home as much of the street as possible. For the Dutchman the street is not hostile, strange and vulgar; it is simply that part of his home which is used in common by himself and his neighbours. In a Dutch street I always enjoy the pleasant and home-like atmosphere. If I want privacy I sit down in the main square of one of the large cities of Holland. I love Holland because she is not a "good-time-country" in the generally accepted sense of the word.

Delft in 1894

From *The World's Famous Places and Peoples: Holland,* by Edmondo de Amicis, translated by Helen Zimmern, published in 1894.

At present Delft is not an industrial or commercial city, and its twenty-two thousand inhabitants live in profound peace. But it is one of the prettiest and most characteristic towns of Holland. The wide streets are traversed by canals shaded by double rows of trees. On either side are red, purple, and pink cottages with white pointing, which seem content in their cleanliness. At every crossway two or three corresponding bridges of stone or of wood, with white railings, meet each other; the only thing to be seen is some barge lying motionless and apparently enjoying the delight of idleness; there are few people stirring, the doors are closed, and all is still.

I took my way toward the new church, looking around to see if I could discover any of the famous storks' nests, but there were none visible. The tradition of the storks of Delft is still alive, and no traveler writes about this city without mentioning it. The new church, founded toward the end of the fourteenth century, is to Holland what Westminster Abbey is to England. The mausoleum of William the Silent is in the middle of the church. It is a little temple of black and white marble, heavy with ornament and supported by slender columns, in the midst of which rise four statues representing Liberty, Prudence, Justice, and Religion.

The Hague

From *Variations on a Dutch Theme* by Peter Temple, reprinted by permission of Martin Secker and Warburg Ltd.

For all its crowds, its searing hubbub of trams and motor traffic, its swarms of harried-looking bicyclists who press through the thoroughfares during the rush hour as densely and purposefully as an invasion of locusts, The Hague still has the air of leisure bequeathed to it since birth. Originally a village round the palace of the Counts of Holland, it has for three hundred and fifty years been the seat of government, the residence of Stadholders and of Royalty.

The cafés round the square opposite the great Hall are crowded with sedate, well-to-do Dutch people, apparently in no hurry whatever; one charming old house, now a place of refreshment, actually calls itself "House of Lords," a resounding title for such an establishment, and one that undoubtedly sets the tone. There is a first-rate club, run on the lines of those declining institutions in Pall Mall, where the attendant who relieves one of hat and coat never gives a check and never makes a mistake, where the food is delicious and the waiting perfect. . . .

The Hague was never a fortified town; there were no walls, and therefore no set bounds to the older part of the city as are found at Amsterdam, which first grew within protecting dykes and, later, walls; or at Leyden, the stronghold clustered into a space made by a division of the Old Rhine; or at Delft, whose boundaries are canals, as is the case in many other of the ancient cities of Holland. In consequence, The Hague has a certain spaciousness round what may be called central precincts, which adds to its leisurely atmosphere.

Canals, Wet Winds and Gables

From *Places,* edited by Geoffrey Grigson and Charles Harvard Gibbs-Smith, reprinted by permission of Hawthorn Books, Inc., all rights reserved.

Haarlem, capital of the province of North Holland, like all Dutch cities, does not seem far from the sea, which is four and a half miles away; it has a sense of wet winds blowing in among its quiet streets, and often in the early evenings a mist blurs the grey-gabled houses along the quays. With Delft it shares a quality of silence—the silence of the narrow canals below arches of foliage, and of the flat tulip fields. It is not perhaps beauty that Haarlem possesses, nor is it anything immediately obvious or compelling. Its topography has been mapped again and again by painters such as Berckheyde, who have recorded for us the space of the Grote Markte, the high shoulder of the fifteenth-century nave of St. Bavo with its spire seeming incongruously short, and the castellated, pinnacled, conglomerate building that is the Town Hall. Haarlem, too, has been painted in blonde tones by Saenredam, the shadows falling across the cobbles, and the gabled houses, snow-laden, steeply rising in a winter sky. But no moods can alter or add to its own somewhat awkward and distinctive charm.

Scheveningen

From *The Netherlands,* edited by Doré Ogrizek, copyright, 1951, by the McGraw-Hill Book Company, Inc., reprinted by permission.

Scheveningen can be compared to a window of The Hague which opens out on the sea; it is a flowery window like all Dutch windows. The road leads through the woods, between villas with an abundance of hollyhocks, larkspur and sage. Then the road finally ends at the long esplanade which overlooks the sands. Spacious hotels and a Kursaal have been built; there are cinemas and tennis courts. The fishing village, which lies at the end of the jetty, near the lighthouse, has changed completely. Simple strongly-built brick houses have replaced the former little houses, but one still sees occasionally young and charming girls wearing the shell-shaped "coiffe" with pleated side-pieces and strange hairpins, in the form of a spiral. Huge carts covered with beautiful rust-colored fishing nets pass by. A smell of sea shells, of foam, spiced with the perfume of sand flowers which adhere to the dunes, makes you hungry and thirsty. . . .

Now Scheveningen is a smart holiday resort and shorts or bathing suits are worn; sunbathing has become the fashion and now one sees rows of oiled bodies against the grey sands. But the beach has kept its huts made out of reeds, its ponies, its slow-moving donkeys. It remains a part of the fashionable Hague with its busy and gay suburbs and its quiet center. Nothing can spoil Scheveningen, not even its dance halls, its cement buildings, its car parks. The beauty of the mornings is unaltered; the quiet of the nights is undisturbed; there remains "the immense sky, the vast sea, and swelling sand dunes and the grey shore. . . ."

Amsterdam, City of Canals

From *Holland,* by E. John Long, copyright, 1955, by Nelson Doubleday, Inc., reprinted by permission.

Amsterdam is unique among the big cities of the world because its town plan has developed in concentric rings of canals that, from the air, look like the growth rings of a giant tree stump. Other canals and waterways cut through these like the spokes of a wheel. Waterways are often more choked with traffic than streets. While Amsterdam's port handles largely domestic trade, it is connected with the North Sea by a broad canal 18 miles long. Since the enlargement of the Ijmuiden lock, the biggest ships afloat can sail inland to Amsterdam's busy wharves. To many visitors, however, Amsterdam is not so much a commercial center as it is one of the great art capitals of the world. Holland's paintings, considered as a whole, are rivaled only by those of Italy and France, and there are those who would rank the Dutch school first. Their Mecca is the Rijksmuseum, with its world-famous collection of Rembrandts, including the "Night Watch," resplendent after its recent cleaning. Here, too, are masterpieces from Frans Hals, Jan Steen, Vermeer, and others too numerous to mention.

Alkmaar, the Friday Cheese Mart

From *Crossroads of the Zuider Zee,* copyright, 1938, by Hendrik de Leeuw, reprinted by permission of J. B. Lippincott Company.

Alkmaar's famous cheese mart takes place just beneath the beautiful *Waag* or Weigh house, where tens of thousands of red-coated round cheeses change hands. To see all the activity from the best place of vantage, one should stand in front of the *Spekbrug* (Bacon bridge). In the canal repose the large wooden barges in whose holds are stacked to the top thousands of cheese balls which are to be traded or have already been traded in. Here one may see hundreds of people from the surrounding towns and villages, the men in long blue and black coats and the women mostly in the characteristic Frisian garb. Some seemed to us quite pretty and wholesome looking, and each one wore the truncated cone of yellow straw bonnet with delicate gold band half an inch wide on the forehead. An unmarried woman wears the band across the temple, extending to the middle of the forehead, while a married woman wears her band of gold on the right, caught beneath a daintily embroidered cap and fastened to a broad gold band by long golden pins, the heads of which are most exquisitely chased or filigreed.

And so the *Mient,* as this large square or cheese mart is called, is filled to the brim with a most colorful gathering of women and men, with the women doing the shopping, especially at the silversmiths, while the men do the bargaining, an art at which these Holland traders are past masters. As soon as the market begins, the cheeses are laid out, like shining yellow globes in straight rows. Trading is done by *handslag* or by a clap of the hands and no contracts are necessary, for a Netherlander's word, sealed by a handclap, is his bond.

On the following double-page spread is a photograph of Stockholm's Town Hall silhouetted at twilight. It is one of the most impressive buildings in all of Europe.

Stockholm's Town Hall

From *Sweden: Model for a World,* copyright, 1949, by Hudson Strode, reprinted by permission of Harcourt, Brace and Company, Inc.

The most impressive building erected in all North Europe in this century is Stockholm's Town Hall. It has made sure a place among the Swedish immortals for its architect, Ragnar Östberg, who first dreamed of such a structure in 1893, began it in 1911, and saw it completed in 1923.

As setting plays an important part in all Stockholm's public buildings, the site of the Town Hall on the island called Kungsholmen could hardly be better. It is so placed on a tip of land thrusting out into Lake Mälaren that it can be seen from most of the wind's twelve directions. By day its splendor is doubled in the mirror of the lake, and at night its illumined outlines are pricked out in rippling gold on the darkened surface of the water. Built of hand-made brick of a mellow russet-red, like some rediscovered from Gustavus Vasa's time, the Stockholm Town Hall is vast in its proportions. At the southeast corner its majestic squarish tower rises three hundred and forty-odd feet, slightly diminishing as it ascends to a belvedere topped with the three golden crowns. . . .

Stockholm, Venice of the North

From *Scandinavia,* edited by Doré Ogrizek, copyright in Great Britain, 1952, reprinted by permission of the McGraw-Hill Book Company, Inc.

"Stockholm-the-city-that-swims-on-the-water," writes Selma Lagerlöf. Seen from an aircraft, or from a magic gander that has rediscovered the secret of flight, the main features of the site certainly gives one the impression that water enters into the very make-up and composition of Stockholm. Here you have Lake Mälaren, there, the Baltic; here a deep-cut bay, there a rocky strait, tracing through the middle of the city a long, royal avenue, dividing it into numerous sections. But go through the place on foot, walking beside canal or creek, and you will feel above all else that you are in a "City-of-air-and-space," worthy of those splendid Swedish athletes, so distinguished both on the track and in cross-country contests through their own forests. This city needs elbow-room. Looking across its streets, one finds the view extended by distant prospects of sky, water and light. "A-city-that-swims-on-the-water?" Rather a city that swims in the landscape, stretching out over it, diving into it. . . .

The title "Venice of the North" should not be rejected, but its exact application needs to be explained. This spacious capital city, imbued with the modern spirit, differs indeed in too many ways from that other island-museum, swarming with people, terrified to change in any detail the plan of its canals and alleys for fear of committing a crime against Art. One must go back in history to the Venice of the early 15th century, animated by the desire to build, to give expression in its monuments to the breadth of its genius. . . .

Lake Vener—Busy Highway of Commerce

From *The World's Great Lakes,* copyright, 1948, by Ferdinand C. Lane, re-printed by permission of the author.

Beautiful Vener . . . situated in southern Sweden is variously spelled Vener and Vanern . . . with an area of 2149 square miles . . . in a region noted for its wild and rugged terrain. The northern shores are rocky and in the main densely forested; the southern lower, more settled, and offering many delight-ful vistas. Among the numerous islands, Lecko in particular is admired for the ancient castle which lends it a medieval glamor.

The major axis of the lake extends some 87 miles from southwest to north-east, while the greatest width is about 44. The deepest recorded sounding is 292 feet. Rocky peninsulas and islands divide the waters into two sections, the smaller lying to the southwest, locally known as Lake Dalbo.

Fish abound and fishing craft add a picturesque touch to the numerous more pretentious trading vessels that ply the surface. For Vener is a busy highway of commerce. From rich deposits to the north come cargoes of iron ore; timber is an important item, as are agricultural and dairy products and a wide variety of manufactured articles. . . . A number of busy ports and manufacturing towns have sprung up along the shores, so that Vener suggests a miniature edition of North America's Great Lakes.

The Heart of Sweden

From *The Icicle in the Sun,* by William Sansom, published by Reynal & Co., Inc., New York, copy-right, 1956, by The Curtis Publishing Company, re-printed by permission of Reynal & Co., Inc., and The Hogarth Press, Ltd.

Often called the heart of Sweden, the province of Dalarna is known abroad as Dalecarlia. Here, in the villages of the long and lovely Lake Siljan, old-fashioned peasant costumes and handicrafts survive more than elsewhere in the country. The usual picture of the broad-hatted, knee-breeched farmer, and of his wife in her striped apron and bodice, will more than likely come from here, and here the fiddlers still gather and the long church boats strike out on the lake. These unusual craft, carrying from fifty to a hundred villagers, gar-landed with green birch leaves and rowed by many white-shirted menfolk, were once the means of visiting the several white churches by the water. But with the advent of roads, they are now used only on ceremonial occasions. However, many of the people still wear the old costumes on Sundays, and though it may sound tourist-inspired to speak of a Dalecarlian walking through the white birch alley in yellow breeches with scarlet pompoms, and his lady in one of her dozen formal costumes (different patterns for funerals, weddings, Christmas and so on), it is not so. They will be at ease, smoking a cigarette, chatting, and in a few seconds the costume is forgotten.

A sight always more startling than a pair of daffodil breeches is the number of white birch trees. This lovely eccentric, with its slender branches that form so exquisite a filigree of silver in the hoarfrost, of misted green in spring, makes one feel as if someone had gone mad with a whitewash brush, splash-ing the dark forest with brilliant streaks of white.

Land of the Midnight Sun

From *Richard Joseph's Guide to Europe and the Mediterranean,* copyright ©, 1956, by Richard Joseph, reprinted by permission of Doubleday & Company, Inc.

You'll find that Norway is one of the great sight-seeing countries of the world. The fjords, which are deep inlets of the sea, extending back into the mountains sometimes for more than a hundred twisting miles, are as much a must for visitors to Norway as the Sphinx and pyramids are to the travelers to Egypt....

If you're in Norway in early summer you have one of the real treats of summer travel waiting for you in the northern part of the country—perpetual sunlight. At least it seems perpetual to the American visitor torn between a desire to see everything while the sun is shining, and his normal behavior pattern of seeking some sleep within every twenty-four hour period. What generally happens is that you keep right on looking as your mail boat pushes its snub little nose into fjord after magnificent fjord until your eyes can see no more and your brain can absorb no further impressions; then you crawl off to your cabin, let the curtains fall across the porthole, and dig your head down under the eiderdown quilt (which covers all Norwegian beds, even in midsummer). You sleep, for a while at least, but you feel guilty, as though you had crawled off to bed at home at high noon, right when something wonderful was about to happen.

Oslo in Winter

From *Norwegian Life and Landscape,* copyright, 1952, by Anthony Martin, reprinted by permission of Elek Books Ltd.

The snow, when it comes, changes the rhythm of the city. There are smiles everywhere and quickened steps. On Sundays and holidays all Oslo, from grandfathers to five-year-olds, takes to the hills. In the morning long queues form outside the railway stations. The girls are dressed in reds and blues and everyone is elated. The skis are strapped to the outside of the coaches which creep like bristling hedgehogs up into the sunshine and the clean air. On the train the talk is technical about the condition of the snow surface and the right grease for the skis. Routes are mapped out in advance and young people think nothing of covering fifty miles while the middle-aged are content to wander comfortably along for twenty miles or so on a Sunday afternoon. During the hours of daylight the city with the slush in the streets is forgotten....

The snow season reaches its climax with the Easter exodus when everyone who can get away spends a skiing holiday in mountain huts and hostels. The Easter holiday is the national festival of the snow, but no stranger who is not proficient in slalom, Telemark swings and Christiania turns should take part. When wet snow flakes drifted down out of an English sky during the war Norwegian exiles were always wistful and intractable. It was something the English could never understand, they said. The first snow of the year is usually a front page story in the Oslo press although it cannot possibly be "news" when the whole town can see that the hills have turned white overnight.

Trondheim

From *All the Best in Scandinavia,* copyright ©, 1949, 1957, by Sidney Clark, reprinted by permission of Dodd, Mead and Company.

It is a very spacious city, with extremely broad thoroughfares and it is still an anomaly for a place of its size, being the last of the wooden cities of the north. Its houses, its business buildings, with few exceptions, and even its royal palace are of wood—and all are painted white.

The palace is used as such only during occasional visits of the king. It is . . . the largest wooden residential building in Scandinavia and local boosters go farther and call it the largest one in Europe.

The hills around Trondheim offer many a beautiful retreat and many a good *utsikt* over city and fjord. One may go by bus to see the little and big *Lerfoss* (falls) or to enjoy the handsomely placed *Lian Restaurant* at the base of the Grakall Mountain. One may take the *Ringbus* from Munkgate to circle the city, partly on high ground. Perhaps best of all, one may climb on foot to the fort called *Kristiansten,* which commands a satisfying hill's eye-view directly down upon the city. If Bergen is the cradle of Norway's modern culture Trondheim is the cradle of Norway herself. The Nid has seen great doings in its day, and its day is by no means over. Two new bridges are getting set to leap across it. Ships of every sort and of many nations tie up at the quays along its banks. It still cuts arabesques through the most important city in the world built on a latitude so far north. Trondheim is but three degrees below the Arctic Circle.

The Open-air Museum of Bygdöy

From *Scandinavia,* edited by Doré Ogrizek, copyright in Great Britain, 1952, reprinted by permission of the McGraw-Hill Book Company, Inc.

I am tempted to say that Bygdöy is the place where you should spend the greater part of your stay in Oslo, for there you will get to know all Norway, as it is represented in the farmsteads that have been brought together. The extent to which the architecture and decoration of these peasant dwellings can be varied may only be known to him who has paid a long, lingering visit to this kind of open-air museum. Adorned with carvings on the outside, and painted on the inside with whimsical, homely or fantastic designs, these wooden houses, differing in style, structure and ornamentation, tell us all about the old life of the distant provinces. They form a village, but a village containing a sample of all that Norway has produced over the centuries, from Telemark right to Finnmark. All the things that filled the houses and illustrate the mode of life of those peasants and farmers are still in their places. There are the musical instruments that enlivened the long winter nights and led the danes in which the young men jumped so high that their shoes touched the rafters. There is the furniture painted in soft colors, the benches and chests carved as they used to carve them in olden days, the neat, gay costumes, the earthenware with all its rustic beauty, the working tools.

31

Copenhagen

From *Denmark,* by Sacheverell Sitwell, published, 1956, by B. T. Batsford Ltd., reprinted by permission.

The capital of Denmark has a prevailing or predominant whiteness. Not only are many of its houses, old and new, whole streets of them, painted white, but there is a white quality in the Danish sunlight, with more than a shade in it of the snows of winter. The white paint of the houses is . . . plain white, sometimes with a tint of grey in it. In the better parts of the town, therefore, it is a white capital. So I remembered it from twenty years before, and so again it proved to be driving down the long straight road into the heart of Copenhagen, through the Town Hall Square, parallel to the Strøget or main shopping street, and at last to Kongens Nytorv with the equestrian statue of the King in the middle and the white-painted Hotel d'Angleterre.

It was pleasant in the morning looking out over the clipped trees to King Christian V on his pedestal, a philoprogenitive monarch in true seventeenth century tradition, and over his head to the masts and white-painted hulls of shipping in Nyhavn, a canal or arm of the harbor which comes right into the far corner of the square. A drawback is the noisiness of the square at night, but one forgets that on a fine morning when drinking the Danish coffee and eating a Danish almond cake. These latter appear with a miraculous freshness every morning, hot and crisp, and must be among the most delicious things it is possible to eat for breakfast.

Tivoli Gardens

From *Denmark Is a Lovely Land,* copyright, 1951, by Hudson Strode, reprinted by permission of Harcourt, Brace & Co.

Right in the city's heart with one side entrance opposite the Central Railway Station and another side entrance facing the Town Hall is the world-famous amusement center of twenty acres called Tivoli. Known as the Capital of Copenhagen, Tivoli has flourished for more than a century. Laid out in 1843 on a part of the town's ancient ramparts and defensive moat, its twenty landscaped acres are the most valuable piece of real estate in the capital. . . .

Where a street carnival may come to an American town once every few years, in Tivoli Gardens it is continuous, resident carnival from the first of May to mid-September. . . . The attractions range from roller coasters, riotous fun fairs, and sundry devices for petty gambling to symphony orchestras and *de luxe* restaurants like Nimb or Wivex or Divan 2, famous for its lobster. Cafés are set in leafy bowers facing artificial lakes. Concerts are given twice a day in a glass pavilion. Dance halls of various categories abound. There is constant entertainment to be had, some for a price, much of it free. It costs nothing to enjoy the outdoor performances of famous European trapeze artists and acrobats. Farm hands from the provinces, bankers, shop assistants, charwomen, diplomats, and ladies-of-fashion, all mingle in pleasant camaraderie. The most lonely person is infected with the crowd's friendliness and gaiety.

Land of Lakes and Forests

From *Scandinavia,* edited by Doré Ogrizek, copyright in Great Britain, 1952, reprinted by permission of the McGraw-Hill Book Company, Inc.

Despite modernization in the sense of mechanization and improved agricultural methods, Finland is still essentially a land of lakes and forests; that is, in fact, the secret of her beauty, unique in the world. A flat country, devoid of high mountains except in a few regions of Lapland—and even there the mountains are high only in comparison with the hills which, elsewhere rise and fall in gentle slopes—a land which impresses the traveler by the intense, constrained poetry of her great expanses of water, by her wealth of lakes connected one to another by rivers or canals, for waterways are highly perfected in Finland. One can wander endlessly from lake to lake—some are divorced from each other only by narrow strips of land—and, seen from the air, the countryside resembles a labyrinth of land and water, inextricably interwoven, giving the earth an extremely curious aspect not found elsewhere, a mysterious charm that holds you in its spell. The play of light on the water is stranger and more beautiful than in any other region of the globe. Between the lakes and rivers stretch immense woodlands, forests of birch, fir and pine, which are at once the beauty and wealth of Finland. This proximity of wooded wastes and highly industrialized civilization gives travelers the impression that the whole of time is contracted into the fleeting present.

On the following double-page spread is a photograph of London's Tower Bridge which spans the Thames. The great towers are joined together with latticed footbridges.

The Thames

From *English Hours,* by Henry James.

I know of no other classic stream that is so splashed about for the mere fun of it. There is something almost droll and at the same time almost touching in the way that on the smallest pretext of holiday or fine weather the mighty population takes to the boats. They bump each other in the narrow, charming channel; between Oxford and Richmond they make an uninterrupted procession. Nothing is more suggestive of the personal energy of the people and their eagerness to take, in the way of exercise and adventure, whatever they can get. I hasten to add that what they get on the Thames is exquisite, in spite of the smallness of the scale and the contrast between the numbers and the space. In a word, if the river is the busiest suburb of London, it is also by far the prettiest.

Architectural Beauties of London

From the foreword by James Pope-Hennessy to *Beautiful London,* published by Phaidon Publishers, Inc., reprinted by permission.

The architectural beauties of London are most often unexpected. They are sometimes hard to find. Not many people know that if you push open the high forbidding wooden gates of the Deanery at St. Paul's, you will find yourself standing in a moss-grown courtyard made dark by plane trees, and facing the dim front of a brick town-house by Sir Christopher Wren. One can wager that many, many Londoners have never seen the sphinxes in Chiswick Park, the Tudor tombs at Stoke Newington, the splendid Norman pillars of Waltham Abbey, the Geffryes workhouses at Shoreditch, the small street sloping down to Saint-Andrew-by-the-Wardrobe, the Italian villas on the Paddington Canal, the little graveyard, feathery with sheep's parsley in summertime, of the Old Church at Edmonton where Charles Lamb lies buried, or that oddest of all Victorial funeral schemes, the Catacombs and Columbarium in Highgate Cemetery. . . .

It is safe to say that the three most famous buildings in England are Westminster Abbey, the Tower of London and St. Paul's Cathedral. It is the Abbey's rich contents, the tomb-figures ranging from the gilt-bronze kings and queens of Plantagenet England, with their tapering fingers and sublime features, and the Torrigiano tomb of the first Tudor, to the gesticulating figures of Roubiliac, that make each visit to it so rewarding. Seen across Parliament Square, the Abbey looks overshadowed by its neo-Gothic neighbour, the New Palace of Westminster. It does not stand out. The outlines of the Tower and St. Paul's, on the other hand, loom along the river, two silhouettes which have come to represent London to people all over the world. The area which these two buildings together dominate—the area of the City, from Blackfriars to Tower Hill—is one in which the feel of old London has lingered longest.

London and the Thames

From *Great Cities of the World,* ed. by William A. Robson, copyright, 1955, by The Macmillan Company, reprinted by permission of The Macmillan Company and George Allen & Unwin, Ltd., London.

London owes much of its size and power to its commanding position astride the Thames . . . The river is navigable for sea-going vessels as far as London, but not much higher. Hence London became a point of trans-shipment from water to land, and from river to sea. Downstream, the river would in past centuries have been impossible to bridge, owing to its great width, and dangerous to ford on account of the heavy tides and broad marshes. The estuary is well placed for ships voyaging to and from the continent. London cannot be attacked or captured from the sea alone, although it could be defended almost entirely by seapower in the days before aviation. There are no physical obstacles to development until one reaches the Chiltern Hills in Hertfordshire or the North Downs in Surrey and Kent.

The London Taxicab

From *Smith's London Journal,* copyright, 1952, by H. Allen Smith, reprinted by permission of the author and Doubleday & Company, Inc.

The London taxicab is a tall, stately, square-looking object with a 1915 air about it and several characteristics interesting to an American. It is engineered so that it could turn around in a broom closet; no matter what its age, it is always glisteningly clean; the neat and comfortable compartment in which the passengers sit is a bad show from the point of view of the rubbernecker—one can't see much of London from it; and the driver is all but isolated from his fare. The glass panel between front and rear usually is open a matter of three inches so the passenger can shout directions, but this arrangement is not conducive to the kind of talk that goes on in a New York taxicab. . . .

Riding these cabs is an experience of great novelty for a New Yorker. It is astonishing to observe the politeness of one driver to another. I had the good fortune to be in a taxi which banged fenders with another taxi close by St. Martin's in the Fields, which is not in the fields. Had this happened in New York the uproar would have been epical—the two drivers would have been out and roaring, each accusing the other of imbecility, each threatening the other with tire tools and uttering sulphuric prose poems. Not in London. I could scarcely believe my senses when the two drivers involved in this small accident began apologizing to each other, both men trying to claim responsibility with no voice raised above a polite conversational tone. As in the case of the ordinary English motorist, they do not curse and growl and scream obscenities back and forth on the streets and highways. . . . In all justice, however, I must report a conversation I had with a London journalist with whom I was riding and who had just nodded politely to a taxi driver who was trying to cut in front of him. I said I thought it a marvelous thing that London drivers don't yell bad words at one another. "It isn't done," he agreed. "But one *thinks* the bad words—one says them back of one's teeth while one is nodding and smiling at the ruddy idiot."

London in Winter

From *London,* by P. G. Wodehouse, copyright ©, 1957, by Saturday Review, Inc., reprinted by permission of the publisher.

If I had a son who had never been abroad and, having touched me for fare and expenses, was planning to visit London, I would say to him "Go there in winter, my boy." Every city has its special season—Paris the spring, New York the fall—and the time to appreciate London is between December and March, when a cozy brown mist hangs over the streets and the sidewalks ooze with a perspiration of mud and water and you see through the haze the welcoming glow of the Bodega lamps, shining like harbor lights. (Not that I specify the Bodega to the exclusion of other and equally worthy hosteleries. All the pubs are good in England's Metropolis.) London resembles the lady of whom Sir W. S. Gilbert wrote in "Trial by Jury" in being seen at its best in the dusk with a light behind it. And the great advantage of being there in winter is that you are not tempted to go away . . . up the river like the three men in the boat, down to Brighton for sea air, or off in your car to one of those stately homes in the country where the Earl or the Duke, if you slip him half-a-crown, will let you potter around and may even lend you a pencil to write "Kilroy Was Here" on the portcullis. . . .

To an American like myself—more the suave, traveled type—there is an abiding fascination in London. I like to saunter hither and thither taking in its quaint sights . . . Whitehall, crowded with mysterious veiled women diffusing a strange exotic scent, on their way to the Foreign Office to steal Naval Treaties . . . Westminster, where the members of Parliament are a never-failing source of entertainment and amusement. (It is forbidden to feed them) . . . St. James's Street and its clubs, the smoking-room windows filled with motionless figures, several of whom have been dead for some days . . . Shepherd's Market, where Michael Arlen's heroines used to parade in green hats . . . Fleet Street, bustling with activity as the journalists—mostly members of the Jukes family—go about their work of getting stories for tomorrow's national daily papers. For, odd as it may seem, papers like the Daily Express are not just Acts of God; they are published deliberately.

Cockney Idylls

From *Round London With the Unicorn,* by G. W. Stonier, published, 1951, by Roy Publishers, reprinted by permission.

First love, first primroses under leaves, the first cuckoo's off-tone third—and the first bus. How hard and resigned, how intent with newspapers, how clean over dirty work suits look the faces! But it's never the first bus. There has always been one a little earlier; and all night, at hourly intervals, buses and trams have been passing. The markets begin to relax: carcase slingers, basket jugglers, squat helmeted fish porters are enjoying a second or third pint. And for every dozen workmen starting the day there is one who has knocked off and, with a yawn, is going home in the sunlight.

The Haunt of Writers—The British Museum

From *The Bookman's London,* copyright, 1951, by Frank Swinnerton, reprinted by permission of Allan Wingate, Ltd., and Doubleday & Company, Inc.

I suppose the most famous London haunt of literary men and women to be the British Museum Reading Room. There, under that enormous dome, at desks radiating from its centre like the spokes of a wheel, sit, hour after hour and month after month, students, scholars, hacks, bibliographers—all to whom continuous reading is a necessity of life. And the setting is worthy of their task. There is a height in this great room, a cathedral-like silence in which a cough or a dropped book echoes and becomes a crime, a monumental air of dignity and opulence in the supply of books, that I have always felt to be inspiring. Not inspiring as natural beauty is inspiring; but scholastically exemplary. One says to oneself: "I *will* learn; I *will* master what I have come here to master." Many must have mastered what they came to master. Not I.

There is a scent of warmth. There are the almost noiseless librarians who slide books on to the desk at one's side. There is that great assembly of catalogues which one draws out by leather loops. And there are the people seated, many of them sprawling, at the desks. They, indeed, are wonderful. Some are precise; they have come for immediate purpose, and they remain only until they have found what they need. Others browse. There are old men who cast aside red mufflers but do not cast aside greatly-worn overcoats; there are those of all ages, seeking "authorities" and material for busy monographs, gratifying the daily needs of editors and publishers, who desire innumerable facts about old books or authors. . . . Lenin is said to have sat there; Swinburne lodged near the Museum; at different times I have met half the literary men of my own era, absorbed and—for a while—happy.

English Trees

From *This England,* copyright, 1936, by Mary Ellen Chase, reprinted by permission of The Macmillan Company.

The best and noblest specimens of English trees stand in green fields or on open hillsides, singly or in small isolated groups like that on St. Catherine's hill, Winchester, with room enough among them to enable each to develop freely on its own lines. To the foreigner walking as he learns to walk, not along the roads, but rather along the paths which intersect the fields everywhere, this quality of English trees is the first to impress itself upon him. Mounting the wooden stiles which, spanning the hedgerows, afford admittance to yet other fields and slopes, he looks across undulating meadows, up hills and down into small valleys, and notes how each tree stands by itself, that oak or elm, that beech or chestnut. Each is an individual, living its own life, careless of its neighbors which never are close enough for annoyance. The green fields encircle each, dotted with grazing cattle and horses. Each receives its own share of rain and rare sunlight. . . .

The Unique Village of Clovelly

From *The West Country,* by R. A. J. Walling, reprinted by permission of Captain R. V. Walling and Messrs. Blackie.

The approach to Clovelly along the cliffs by the three miles of the Hobby Drive is an enchantment. How startling the contrast between this cliff scenery and the stark rocky sea-face of Lynton or Ilfracombe!

For here, instead of naked rock, "behold," as Kingsley said, "a forest-wall, five hundred feet high, of almost semi-tropical luxuriance." The effect of this mist of greenery, whencesoever seen, is strange in the extreme, and most of all from the sea. It may remind any who have lain off shore at Orotava of the mossy looking forests clothing the steep sides of the foothills beyond the peak of Teneriffe. And in the midst of it occurs Clovelly, that strangest village in all England, the *clove-lea,* the cleft in the rock, the little aperture in the forest wall, up which a tiny street of houses climbs at such an angle that no roadway can be made upon it, but only a flight of steps, where no vehicle can travel, and he who would ride must perforce go on donkey-back.

The little harbor (built long ago by the Carys of Clovelly Court), the few houses at the bottom of the cleft, the cottages covered with climbing plants, the green shade all around—these things have been painted and picture-postcarded and prose-poemed till one might fancy the very name of Clovelly hackneyed beyond endurance. But Clovelly survives it all. Clovelly cannot be overpraised, because the reality of it will not yield to adulation in words. It cannot be spoiled, because it is unique: it comes as a fresh wonder at every revelation; it cannot be altered or extended, because there is no room for growth.

The Lake District

From *A Prospect of Britain,* by Andrew Young, published by Harper & Brothers, reprinted by permission of the publishers.

It was after his visit to the Lake District, and with special reference to it, that Nathaniel Hawthorne wrote: "I shall always be glad of this tour, and shall wonder the more at England, which comprehends so much, such a rich variety, within its little bounds." But while the Lake District contains much, much more, than any other part of England of a corresponding size, compactness in itself would not distinguish it from certain parts of the Highlands; what does distinguish it is the kind of compactness, so great a variation in so small a compass. Dale differs from dale; they are of the same genus, but different species. The mountains do more than differ from each other; they are Protean, changing their shapes according to the view-point, so that, however familiar they are, they may be difficult to identify. Uplands contrast with lowlands, the stern austerity of the fells with the Arcadian charm of the dales. Yet with all this variety you get the impression of a cheerful united country; there is a friendliness among its parts, that on a fine day you feel is extended to yourself.

The Conspicuous Town

From *Summer in Scotland,* by Ivor Brown, published, 1952, by Collins, reprinted by permission of the publishers.

Well did Marjorie Fleming call Edinburgh "The Conspicuous Town." You see it from the country surrounding as well as from its own sheer hills. It is the natural capital of a divided country, since it embodies both Highland and Lowland; the Castle Rock might have been carved out of Glencoe, yet the Lothian coast has as serene a tilth and as sweet a set of links as ever cried out for a plough on the one hand and a golf-club on the other. Poised on its own ridges as it is, as James Bone has said, "less the handiwork of man than a rearrangement of Nature." And that is what a fine town should be, a marriage of the natural with the invented. Yet it caters solidly for all needs, not the aesthetic only, and has a particular knack of making all that it offers for sale look even more attractive than it would do anywhere else. We live in an age of standardized goods: no doubt any other large city can supply in its shops of quality much the same stuff at much the same prices. Yet in Edinburgh something seems to be added—I am not referring to the costs of a shopping excursion—and your appetite for buying is strangely quickened. It is the genius of the place to raise ordinary things to a higher power.

Edinburgh, The Athens of the North

From *Scotland,* by Evelyn Irons, copyright ©, 1957, by Nelson Doubleday, Inc., reprinted by permission.

The Edinburgh Festival, started as an experiment in 1947, brings thousands of visitors to Scotland's capital for three weeks in late August and early September. It is an international festival of the arts, but Scottish playwrights and players, musicians and artists, are taking a bigger part in it each year, and Edinburgh, known in Sir Walter Scott's early nineteenth-century days as The Athens of the North, is once more a great Scottish cultural center: many young local artists and poets live there instead of migrating to London or Paris, as so many of their predecessors have done.

The view from Princes Street, across the misty gardens and the deep ravine of a railroad cutting, to the Old Town on the ridge beyond, with its jumbled tenements raking the skyline and Edinburgh Castle jutting from its basalt rock, is as dramatic as the first sight of the New York skyscrapers from an incoming liner. Princes Street, often called the handsomest street in Scotland, is not all that beautiful in detail. Architecturally, it is quite an ordinary shopping street, except that it has the shops on one side only, with the opposite side open to the view of the Castle. The one notable building—the Register House, designed by eighteenth-century Scotsman Robert Adam, one of the two world-famous Adam brothers—is dwarfed by an unbeautiful railway hotel. But the whole effect is impressive just the same. This side of the town is "New" Edinburgh, much of it laid out in rectangular blocks and classical squares more than a century ago.

Sir Walter Scott's Abbotsford

From *Your Trip to Britain,* by Richard Joseph, copyright, 1952, by Richard Joseph, published by Doubleday & Co., Inc., reprinted by permission.

Abbotsford is Sir Walter Scott's estate, on a slope descending to the River Tweed, and where he lived from 1812 until his death in 1832. A new wing has been added and a few alterations and restorations made, but the house you'll see is substantially the same as it was in Scott's day—a baronial mansion of many turrets, perhaps a bit cranky in its architecture, since it was built over a period of about ten years in direct accordance with his whims. Actually, Abbotsford turned out to be a bit of a white elephant for Scott. He sank so much money into building it and filling it with his great collection of Scottish historical relics (the keys to Loch Leven Castle, which were thrown into the loch on Queen Mary's escape, the gun of Rob Roy, etc.) that despite the ceaseless activity of his pen he found himself continually dogged by debt. The happy ending to the story is that, in recognition of his great gift to Scottish letters, his creditors presented Abbotsford to the bankrupt Sir Walter, free of debt. Two and a half miles east of Abbotsford is Scott's "Fair Melrose" a little town situated in lovely surroundings overlooking the River Tweed, with the graceful Eildon Hills rising in the background. . . . Melrose is famous for its beautiful ruined church of a twelfth-century Cistercian monastery, so romantically described in Scott's *Lay of the Last Minstrel.* Buried beneath its high altar is the heart of the Scottish hero-king, Robert the Bruce.

The Highlands

From *Scotland,* by Neil M. Gunn, in *Holiday,* copyright ©, 1950, by The Curtis Publishing Company, reprinted by permission of Brandt & Brandt.

It is natural to attribute romance to the Highlands because in itself it is so varied and beautiful a country. There are bare gaunt regions with outcrops of the oldest rock in the world, the earth's original crust. Glens with birches and tumbling streams and blue lochs. Mountain chains range most ways, yet the highest peaks are not much over 4000 feet, so that they never lose a certain intimacy. They can be encompassed, and many of them, like the Cuillin in the island of Skye, set problems for roped climbers than have given them a wide fame. The hills and moors for the greater part are heather clad and divided into great sporting estates, where grouse are shot over trained dogs and, in the higher reaches, red deer are stalked. The rivers abound in trout and salmon.

Slantwise across this country stretches the Caledonian Canal, from Fort William in the southwest to Inverness in the northeast: an attractive excursion for any visitor, that can be savored the better from the deck of a boat, sailing through many lochs with wooded hillsides, and being stepped up or down at the various nests of locks. One of the lochs, twenty-four miles long, is called Loch Ness—where the Monster lives.

The Dublin Horse Show

From *James Reynolds' Ireland,* copyright by James Reynolds, 1953, and reprinted by permission of Farrar, Straus and Cudahy, Inc.

It is an event unique in this world, surely. For many reasons the show is different from other outdoor events of this nature. The Horse Show grounds at Ballsbridge are magnificently landscaped. Flowers are everywhere. The first glimpse one gets from the broad street which passes in front of the Georgian Façade of the main building seems a shade formal and cold. Once one passes the turnstile, the color and warmth of the booths offering homespuns, divers coloured Donegal and Leenane tweeds, riding boots and breeches, rat-catcher jackets and beautifully tailored side-saddle habits of charcoal gray or dark blue, engulf one in friendliness. Bars galore beckon the thirsty. Restaurants both under the trees and inside offer the best and freshest Irish food. The Horticultural Hall is as dazzling as Aladdin's cave where flowers play the part of jewels. Then the next step is to roam along the alleys where hunters of every age and performance are being groomed or contentedly munching.

Outside there are four spacious rings surrounded by gabled buildings of black and white half-timbering. Trees shade the walks. One may stand in shade at the rails while the contestants for various hunter class honors show in the sun. These morning classes are well attended, but many persons prefer to go across the roadway to the Goff Sales of yearlings. These sales alone attract horsemen and women from all over the world. Often 175 yearlings are sold in a morning. Some of the most famous winners in England, India, France, Belgium, Italy, North and South America, and Australia have been purchased from vendors at these sales.

O'Connell Street

From *The Silent Traveller in Dublin* by Chiang Yee, reprinted by permission of The John Day Company.

I treated O'Connell Street as itself one of the chief sights of Dublin and strolled on both sides of it for hours at a time. It is a very wide street, and has the look of the Champs Elysees minus the trees or of Whitehall with splendid shops instead of official buildings. To my nose, what seemed an abnormally large number of icecream shops breathed out the smell of Broadway. But such comparisons are invidious. O'Connell Street has a character all its own; I could feel it especially when I stood on O'Connell Bridge. The bridge is as wide as the street. In addition to traffic lanes for buses, trams and cars, it has waiting-stands some yards away from the pavement along the handsome balustrade on either side. Although O'Connell Street is the busiest street in the city and its traffic is always heavy, one can walk quite at ease to the centre of the bridge and stand there near a lamp-post gazing around without fear of being knocked down or thrown over into the river. And the traffic seemed quietened when going over the bridge, though the drivers did not appear to slacken their speed, an impression I have not had on any other bridge in the world. Perhaps Dublin's soft air was responsible for my illusion.

An Tostal

From *The South and The West of It,* © copyright, 1956, by Oriana Atkinson, reprinted by permission of Random House, Inc.

When Miss Witlov and I were in Dublin, the city was decorated within an inch of its life in honor of An Tostal (At Home), Ireland's spring festival, and very pretty it looked, tóo. All the tall street lights were garlanded with living flowers. The parks and open squares had special displays of tulips and other spring blooms. The hotels and some of the public buildings were draped with bright bunting and it all gave an air of real festivity to the place.

This spring festival has been an annual event for four years now. It is advertised as a nation-wide celebration in which all Ireland participates. But if you have the idea that it is a big, noisy affair, with brass bands blaring and people filling the streets with shouts and song, you are mistaken. It's not at all like the New Orleans Mardi Gras. And it's not quite like the story Sean O'Casey tells about it, either. He says that once, during the first festival, a tourist asked a Dubliner where the festival was. The Dublin man, who had not been aware that there *was* a festival, was nonplused. Not liking to disappoint a visitor, however, he said, "Oh, sure, I think it's just down at the end of the street." It's a nice, gentle little festival and you can take it or leave it alone. There are sports events and art exhibits, and folk music and dancing. Tickets for these are on sale at all the hotels, and the Irish Transport Company has inaugurated special tours around the country that include many of the An Tostal features.

The Blarney Stone

From *Lovely Is the Lee,* copyright, 1945, by Robert Gibbings, reprinted by permission of E. P. Dutton & Company, Inc., and J. M. Dent & Sons, Ltd.

Cities of the world depend for their fame on piles of stones, scattered or in order, but this village, where naught but tweeds are made, rests all its fame upon a single stone. That stone is in the parapet of the castle, Blarney Castle, built in the fifteenth century of Cormac MacCarthy, whose genealogy will be found in Keating's *History of Ireland,* ascending through Heber the Fair, son of Milesius, the Spanish hero, up to the patriarch Noah himself, not a link in the chain missing.

On arrival at the castle, the pilgrim climbs to its battlemented summit, and having handed any loose valuables that might be in his pockets to a friend, lowers himself head first between parapet and main building. Thus he is able to add one more kiss to that stone already highly polished by the lips of votaries. Although the present owner of the castle has very kindly put iron bars for the convenience of visitors it is nevertheless wise to have at least two friends holding on to your shins during the operation. Not that anything very serious can happen. The last man who fell, eighty feet into the tree below, was able to report for duty next day.

Trinity College

From *As I Was Going Down Sackville Street*, copyright, 1937, by Oliver St. John Gogarty, reprinted by permission of Oliver D. Gogarty.

The way through the Front Gate divides the great quad of Trinity College, which opens on a large cobbled space on the third side, into two equal squares. In the lawn of each stands a great oak. Old grey houses with windows framed in lighter stone shelter the immense trees. In front, the graceful campanile stands between the library and the Graduates' Memorial, backed by two lawns and the Queene Anne Wing. Nearer, the Chapel faces the Examination Hall. Equal lawns intervene. It took me a long time to accept the intrusion of red brick among the grey walls, but now it lends a warm background to the campanile and tones with the pink hawthorns in the grassy spaces. Is there any College in the world that for its size has sent within the few centuries since it was founded more famous men near and far? I asked. Sterne, Burke, Goldsmith, Hamilton of Quaternion fame, Fitzgerald who anticipated Marconi and was the first who had the courage to put his convictions of flight to the test in a glider from the parapet of the Engineering School. Her degrees are honored farther afield than many colleges go.

Untidy undergraduates were grouped about the chains. Lady undergraduates unwilling to relinquish cap and gown floated across the path. Left and right the dark portals of the house gloomed sullenly. That one over there, the last next to the Examination Hall, leads to the Provost's house, but no figure emerges. . . . We pass under the Library, one of the five great Libraries which can lay claim to a free copy of every book printed of Great Britain or Ireland. We passed the results of Ruskin's *Stones of Venice,* the Engineering School. They were open to intimations in those days. A beautiful building—perhaps the most beautiful modern building in Dublin. The sweet smell of new-mown grass flowed from the spacious Park.

On the following double-page spread is a photograph of the beautiful St. Bartholomew's Chapel on the Königssee, Bavaria, a region noted for its magnificent lakes, mountains.

The Königssee and St. Bartholomew's Chapel

From *Germany,* edited by Doré Ogrizek, copyright in Great Britain, 1956, reprinted by permission of the McGraw-Hill Book Company, Inc.

From the moment the motor launch takes off across the dark waters between steep banks, the burden of the primitive world seems to weigh upon your shoulders. The colors and shapes, and the peaks that loom up behind the range of rocks seem to have been created with the sole aim of luring you into the nether regions. And whilst the pale green meadows fringing the bank gradually draw nearer, and the bulb-shaped tower of St. Bartholomew's chapel introduces a bright and reassuring note, the giant wall of the Watzmann-Wand looms up before your eyes. Although this hostile world has doubtless long been vanquished by mountaineers, a shiver of terror runs down your spine at the sight of the brutal beauty of Nature untamed. Myriads of tourists have a gloomy foreboding when they set off in quest of sensations beside the Königssee—and few of them return reassured. It is not surprising that the Berchtesgaden region abounds in legends and ancient practices. The horn of the "Little Watzmann" and the crests of the neighboring rocks represent the family of King Watzmann who was turned to stone with all his kith and kin in punishment for his evil deeds. To the north, so they say, Charlemagne is still alive, imprisoned in a cave.

Rhineland Is Wineland

From *The Wines of Germany,* by Frank Schoonmaker, copyright, 1956, by Frank Schoonmaker, published by Hastings House, Publishers, reprinted by permission.

"Rhineland," says the old German proverb, is "wine-land," and certainly, as far as Germany is concerned, this is gospel. Every German wine of the slightest consequence, from the *Drachenblut,* that rather anemic "Dragon's Blood" which the slopes of *Drachenfels,* near Bonn, yield in the north, to the pleasant little *Seeweine* produced on the shores of Lake Constance on the south, is, in the last analysis, a Rhine wine, or at least a wine produced in the Rhine basin. . . .

Most of this vineyard country, oddly enough, has a trace or a whiff of a what-you-will of Southern Europe in its make-up. The villages are typically and charmingly German, with half-timber houses and high gables, old, painted wrought-iron signs over the tavern doors, ruined castles on a good many of the hills, and windowboxes full of flowers along every main street of every important town. And yet this feeling of the South persists—you will see fig trees and almond trees and apricot trees in the sheltered gardens. . . . Constantly, and almost everywhere, you will find something reminiscent of Northern Italy or Southern France or Spain, and even now, after eighteen hundred years, something that will make you remember that most of this Rhine country, this vineyard country, was once part of the Roman Empire, influenced by Latin customs and subject to Roman law. . . . There is, in the life of this wine country, something ancient and good, a feeling of an old civilization, of well-tilled and well-loved soil.

The Black Forest

The Black Forest is both a mountain chain and a concept. As a range it belongs to the former Land Baden extending from Karlsruhe down to the Swiss frontier. As a concept it belongs to the world, if not for its spas then because of its cuckoo clocks, samples of which have traveled as far as the Antipodes.

It deserves its name. The typical tree here is the silver fir standing in neat tightly packed rows. It is dark in these woods, for the light filters sparsely through the thickset crowns. It is still, for the soft soil absorbs the sound of your footsteps and muffles the odor of resin and rich rotting earth, and there is life, expressed in the shadowy movements of a restless animal world: squirrels busy on the grounds, a badger slipping into hiding, a woodpecker spiraling up a tree, and, toward evening, deer crossing your path on their way to a clearing.

The deep dark woods are a main characteristic of the Black Forest, but the range is more than one hundred miles long and over forty miles broad, and within the space of its wide expanse there are many things for the tourist to see and enjoy. There are deep-cleft valleys and softly contoured mountain tops, alpine pastures and fern- and flower-encircled lakes, and timbered houses with roofs hanging low to the ground, and people in folk dress, people engaged in cutting gems or building organs or carving clocks. There are museums to see and ruins of castles and cloisters and small medieval craft centers with their ancient gates and walls intact. With all that, you have the choice of dozens of well-organized summer and winter resorts and some of Germany's best spas whose springs were known to the Romans and whose hotels have given satisfaction to princes and kings.

On the following double-page spread is a photograph of the city of Salzburg, renowned for its wonderful music festival, and the Hohensalzburg, a medieval fortress.

49

Wolfgangsee and Michael Pacher's Altar

From *All About Austria,* by Virginia Creed, copyright, 1950, by Duell, Sloan & Pearce, Inc., reprinted by permission.

St. Wolfgang . . . is a Salzkammergut highlight. The real name of the lake here is the Abersee, but that is forgotten, the town of St. Wolfgang having now given its name to the lake too. The shores of the Wolfgangsee are formidable; great gray mountains crowd right down to them, leaving no space for flowery meadows. The terrible wall of the Totesgebirge ('Mountain of Death') juts out into the horizon, and the Schafberg looms above. This setting, however, is in sharp contrast with a life known from New York to Tokyo for its lighthearted gaiety. The combination of fashionable and peasant high jinks in St. Gilgen and the worldwide popularity of the much performed and translated operetta *White Horse Inn* have given the Wolfgangsee a well-justified reputation. . . .

In true Austrian fashion, it is only a step from the terrace of the White Horse Inn to the church of St. Wolfgang. Through the rounded yellow arches of the cloistered way the view of lake and mountain is incomparable. The Benedictine monk, St. Wolfgang, founded the church when Christianity was new. It is beautiful in its exterior simplicity, very holy to pilgrims, and contains one of the most exquisite and highly prized art treasures of the Western world: the masterpiece of the fifteenth-century woodcarver, Michael Pacher of South Tyrol. Students of art and the Gothic age come from everywhere to study and sketch this altar.

Vienna in Winter

From *Vienna,* by Joseph Wechsberg, copyright ©, 1956, by Saturday Review, Inc., reprinted by permission of the publisher.

Some people love Vienna best in the dead of winter, when the city's baroque grandeur and Gothic façades are screened by a slight haze that softens the contours and mercifully conceals the symptoms of elegant decay. Like the *pourriture noble* grapes of Chateau d'Yquem, Vienna is sweet, soft, and slightly overripe. Older people love the afternoons when it gets dark early and the squares, palaces, and monuments of Hapsburg emperors stand silent under white curtains of softly falling snow flakes. That, the old-timers say, is the perfect moment for nostalgia and dreaming about a past that seems so remote now that some wonder whether it ever was. It is also the moment when everybody in Vienna who can afford it—and a great many who can't—go to their favorite coffeehouse to talk, read, or just sit and gaze into blue smoke over a cup of their favorite beverage: twenty-eight different shades from *Schale Gold* to *Kapuziner,* but always the flavor of fine coffee.

Vienna's main attractions are indoors: opera and music, whipped cream and *Wiener Schnitzel,* waltz and schmaltz. Even the great outdoors attraction —the *Heuriger* wine garden is now an all-year-round business, and the new wine or what passes for it is served in well-heated, wood-panelled rooms.

Pearl of Mountain Provinces

Going east into the Tyrol you must pass by railroad through a six-mile tunnel or drive over the spectacular Arlberg Pass, 6000 feet high. Either way, Tyrol is worth the journey, and you will not be surprised to learn that this province of rustling forests, picturesque mountain villages, and incomparable ski slopes attract nearly a million tourists each year.

Tyrol is famous for its national costumes and its handicrafts dating back to the Middle Ages. These can best be appreciated in the extensive collection of furniture and folk art in the Folk Museum at Innsbruck, the provincial capital. The Tyrolese, noted for their love of music and yodeling, are especially proud of their national hero, Andreas Hofer, an innkeeper who stood up to Napoleon like David confronting Goliath, and actually inflicted two defeats on his troops in the Tyrolean war of liberation in 1809. A huge bronze statue of this doughty innkeeper stands on the Berg Isel outside Innsbruck. A smaller statue in the Hofkirche is draped perpetually in black because Andreas Hofer's homeland, the South Tyrol, was awarded to Italy after the first world war.

Arlberg—The Skier's Paradise

To every skier the name Arlberg is magic—white magic. The name derives from a connecting link between Tyrol and Vorarlberg, as well-known in Medieval times as it is today. The approach to the "Temple of the White Art," as skiing is called with reverence hereabouts, is through narrow passes glinting with black and white marbled bark of silver birches. Anyone who has spent a fortnight at St. Anton, Lech, or Zurs, all admired winter sports resorts, will agree that it is a never-to-be-forgotten experience. The winding pass of Klostertal is a tortuous way, a maze of viaducts, tunnels and breath-taking curves, but if the trip can be managed the scenic splendor, winter or summer, is too exciting to be foregone.

Langen-on-the-Arlberg is the axis for any number of rewarding excursions into the land of sky and mountains. One particular favorite of mine is the great Walser Valley, the villages of crosshatched larchwood houses hardly distinguishable from the sun-scorched grasses and amber moss sheathing the rocks. Here is the land of the avalanches, a spectacular winter force in the Arlberg. Late spring is their crashing time when snow, which sometimes does not entirely disappear during the summer, is carved into improbable shapes by the moving sabers of ice. One's imagination takes wings as the eye traces palaces and pavilions, snow galleons sailing rippled seas and whole cavalcades of gigantic knights in armor, thrashed up against the blue sky, only, perhaps, to be assailed by another avalanche and tossed crashing into deep ravines, the black rocks glistening with ice spray.

Zurich, City of Finance and Beauty

From *Footloose in Switzerland,* copyright, 1952, by Horace Sutton, reprinted by permission of Rinehart & Company, Inc.

Zurich has been, during various interludes in its history, the favorite city of such variegated personalities as Charlemagne, James Joyce and Richard Wagner and a band of refugees who washed up on its city limits during World War II. For all its fascination with finance, Zurich is a city of great beauty. The Zurichsee is a reservoir for the River Limmat, which splits the city's ancient quarter and slips past the old façades of the guildhouses to spread finally into the Aare. The houses and the hotels of Zurich squat all around the corner of the Lake of Zurich, which in summer is speckled with white and red sails and paddle boats and swans. . . .

After a sail, or a speedboat ride, or a steamer trip up to Rapperswil, a small town on the lake, you can sit at the Bauschänzli, a beer garden that was once a waterside fort, and watch the summer evening invade the bright afternoon.

The cocktail hour is handsomest in Zurich at Baur au Lac, a magnificent hotel, one hundred fifty yards from the lake's edge. . . . A ten-piece orchestra in blue blazers edged in white, left over from a Scott Fitzgerald party, plays a mixture of Italian, German, French, and American tunes. Over it all hangs a cloud of air once fresh out of the Alps, now perfumed with the smoke of Melachrinos mixed with the essence of Femme de Marcel Rochas.

Lake Leman

From *Switzerland,* edited by Doré Ogrizek and J. G. Rufenacht, copyright, 1949, by the McGraw-Hill Book Company, Inc., reprinted by permission.

Lake Leman, sometimes called the Lake of Geneva, has always held a tremendous attraction for poets and writers of all nationalities. It was on its shores, by Montreux, that J. J. Rousseau placed the unhappy love story of "La nouvelle Heloise." And Lord Byron always found solace for his distracted nerves in the silence of "clear, placid Leman."

The surface of Lake Leman, reflecting on the north the sloping vineyards of the canton of Vaud, and on the south the chestnut groves and pastures of Savoy, is 1220 feet above the level of the sea. Its area of 224 square miles makes it the largest lake in Switzerland, while the Rhone, descending from the Valais, furnishes it with 70% of its water, drawn from a surface of many hundreds of square miles of glaciers and snow. Yet Lake Leman itself never freezes except in certain small, very restricted areas. Consequently there is a fairly southern type of climate on its shores, and the powerful radiations from its surface in autumn help ripen the grapes in the vineyards. This is one important reason why in this countryside all other crops have been sacrificed to the vine. Along the lakeside between Geneva and Lausanne lie charming villages and lovely country estates. Several of the villages, such as Nyon, Rolle and Morges, have their own castles and any one of them provides an ideal setting for a quiet and restful vacation.

The Matterhorn

From *Zermatt and the Valais,* by Sir Arnold Lunn, reprinted by permission of Hollis & Carter Limited.

It is, perhaps, from just above Zermatt, from the Riffelalp, that the Matterhorn is seen to greatest advantage. The gentle walk from the Riffelalp station to the hotel is one of the loveliest of Alpine rambles, and the view of the Matterhorn showing between the pines has no rivals. The impression produced is due not only to the power and the glory of this most majestic of peaks, but also to the delicate details, the suggestion of a breaking wave in the summit crest, the white sweep, like a bridal train, of the Stockje ice-slope, the lovely curve of the ridge which stoops from "the Shoulder," and "the Shoulder" itself, that subtle intrusion of snow into massive complexities of rock.

The great mountain long remained unconquered because it was protected not only by its natural difficulties but also by adventitious terrors. In the Italian valley of Breuil, the Becca, as the Matterhorn was called, was the theme of many legends. Mothers would frighten their children by the threat that the wild man of the Becca would carry them away, and they would tell how Gargantua, a giant in Aosta, strode across the range of peaks which divides Italy from Switzerland, in far-off times a uniform ridge instead of, as now, a series of peaks. As the giant stood with one foot in Italy, and the other in Switzerland, the surrounding rocks fell away, and the pyramid of cliffs caught between his legs alone remained standing. Thus was the Matterhorn born.

Majesty of the Jungfrau

From *The Alps, The Danube, and The Near East,* by Frank G. Carpenter, copyright, 1924, by Carpenter's World Travels, reprinted by permission of Frances Carpenter Huntington and Doubleday & Company, Inc.

I have seen most of the great mountain views of the world, but none which, for sheer beauty, surpasses that of the Jungfrau. I have stood on Tiger Hill near Darjeeling and watched the sun gild the top of Mt. Everest, the loftiest mountain on earth. Everest is almost three miles higher than the Jungfrau, but the effect from Tiger Hill is somewhat spoiled by distance and by the lower peak of Kunchinjinga, which stands in the foreground obstructing the view. From the bronze statue of Christ that marks the boundary between Argentina and Chile I have seen Aconcagua, the highest of the Andes. It is almost two miles higher than where I am now, but like Mt. Everest, it is dwarfed by its surroundings. I have seen Mt. McKinley from the heights of Alaska and I know Fujiyama, the snowy symmetrical cone which the Japanese worship. Each has its own beauties, but none has a more beautiful setting than the Jungfrau, the Virgin of the Alps. Whether viewed from the valley, or here face to face, she has a majesty all her own. . . .

Basle

From *The World's Famous Places and Peoples: The Rhine,* by Karl Stieler, translated by G. C. T. Bartley, published in 1898.

The very first effect of Basle, as it lies on both sides of the Rhine, is striking and varied. Nature and history, and not simply accident and population, have formed it into a town. It could not help becoming what it has. There is every development of natural power, and the charm of this impression is increased by the antique historical character on which its present condition is based. The prosperity of Basle has been handed down for centuries. Of late handsome villas have been built in the suburbs; but the older parts of the town remain as they have been for hundreds of years, and the old-fashioned burgher character runs through the nature of the people, and holds them fast to their liberties.

The Rhine was the great storehouse from which the town drew its wealth, and became what it was. It was the Rhine that carried thousands of foreign guests and foreign treasures to Basle. A regular water traffic was established between Basle and Strasbourg as early as the sixteenth century, when long caravans of merchants were still wearily dragging along the high-road. The paving of the streets began in 1417. The old Rhine town was always proud of its name, and the bold struggles it made would vie with many a city in which princes raised their thrones.

Bernese Bears

From *Switzerland,* by Alice Taylor, copyright, 1955, by Nelson Doubleday, Inc., reprinted by permission.

Bern, capital of Switzerland and seat of the federal government since 1848, is the center of one of the richest farming areas in the country, yet it does not rank as a large commercial city. People go there, rather, to see its ancient streets that curve gracefully with the bend of the Aar River, the sidewalks covered with arcades, the lovely fountains, the bears that decorate so many buildings, the live ones in the Bear Pit, and the magnificent view of the Jungfrau.

In the old days the Bernese were famous soldiers, who fought in many regiments abroad. Now they have a reputation for being prudent, honest, conservative, and rather slow-moving—somewhat like their beloved bears, which have been favorites for a long time since they first appeared on the town seal back in 1224. Bears are also a prominent feature of the famous clock installed in 1530 in the Clock Tower on the Kramgass. To see them in action you should arrive three or four minutes before the hour. A rooster crows first, then some little bears appear and go around in a circle, a cock crows again, and a little man holding a staff and an hourglass strikes the hours. Simultaneously, in the belfry at the top of the Tower, a figure in armor strikes the hours on a great bell with a hammer.

SOUTHERN EUROPE
AND AFRICA

On the following double-page spread is a photograph of the fishing village and resort of Tossa de Mar on Spain's rugged and picturesque Costa Brava.

KRONFELD © PAA

The Costa Brava

From *All About Spain,* by Georgia Long, copyright, 1951, by Duell, Sloan & Pearce, Inc., reprinted by permission.

The road from Barcelona to the French border is one series of scenic surprises. This part of Spain is called the Costa Brava (Rugged Coast), and as you drive along it constantly changes from mountains, cliffs, and rocks to beaches, fields, and calm backwaters. Known only to discriminating persons, this part of Spain is still "undiscovered." All along the shore are historical monuments and old inscriptions cut into the rocks—mute evidences of the Phoenician, Greek, and Roman civilizations, for they have been left by ships which put into these ports. The stones of the forts and the many monasteries tell us of times of strife and faith. At Blanes are pine trees; at Lloret, beaches; at Tossa del Mar, walls and ramparts; while at San Feliu, with its maze of steep streets, coral was taken out of the sea for the first time in history, in the 15th century. Beyond Palamos, a cork-exporting port, the terrain becomes more gentle, the sky a pure blue with indescribable light effects.

S'Agaro, only a mile from San Feliu, the most important town of the Costa Brava, is the site of an ideal town which exemplifies the finest modern planning. In Roques Planes, Madeleine Carroll has built a house, and other well-known artists have found peaceful retreats in the vicinity. One characteristic of the Costa Brava which is seen nowhere else except in California is the pine trees growing so close to the sea. They have the same umbrella-like shapes and contours made by the wind.

Madrid in Winter

From *Madrid,* by Barnaby Conrad, copyright ©, 1957, by Saturday Review, Inc., reprinted by permission of the publisher.

Someone has noted so well: If you can't stand food cooked in olive oil, or the most damnably irregular hours for eating and sleeping in the civilized world, or a total contempt for punctuality, then don't go to Madrid. However, if you would like the handsomest European capital outside of Paris, the most hospitable people in the world, and a charming fifty-years-behind-times atmosphere, then Madrid is the place for you, summer or winter. Sacheverell Sitwell has written: "Perhaps no foreigner who has ever been touched by Spain is ever quite the same again." And Madrid is Spain; not the colorful picture postcard Spain that is Sevilla; nor the progressive, modern Spain that is Barcelona, but the true heart and soul of the country. . . .

What is there for the winter tourist in Madrid? It is true that Spain is famous and justly so for its spring and summer festivals, its bullfights, and its religious pageants. These more or less disappear from October until Holy Week. But the permanent attractions which have lured visitors for centuries to the Iberian Peninsula remain. . . . Some of the greatest of Spain are to be seen in or near Madrid: El Escorial, which is certainly one of the wonders of the world; the incomparable El Prado museum; and nearby the town of Toledo, whose picturesque artistry competes with the attraction of its numerous El Grecos.

The Fair in Seville

From *Kings Without Castles,* copyright ©, 1957, by Lucy Herndon Crockett, reprinted by permission of Rand McNally & Company, Publishers.

I think that Seville's *feria* must be the world's gayest and most romantic event. No American girl could be blamed for being taken with the olive-skinned *caballeros* who in dashing *cordobés* hats, short jackets, and tooled Andalusian chaps ride dainty Arab mounts, right hands resting lightly on their hips in a gesture ineffably *seigneur,* their flashing eyes roving complacently over the heads of such drab onlookers as myself . . .

. . . or for envying the Sevillanas mounted gracefully behind them, each with a bared arm around the slender waist of her young horseman, the enormous flounced skirt draped over the entire rear half of the horse. Unutterably charming; and perhaps the last living evidence of medieval chivalry to persist, wholly without affectation, into the twentieth century.

For seven days the music doesn't stop. In the open-faced *casetas* lining the gaudy fairways the dancers dip and whirl in the graceful *sevillana* that goes on endlessly, in spontaneous combustion breaking out even in the streets. At 4:00 a.m. in my bed far from the fairgrounds I could still hear, down the courtyard shaft, the restless sound of castanets. Next to the daily prelunch parade of prancing horses and mule-drawn carriages I was enchanted by the children who matched their elders in dancing as though bewitched. The full, flounced skirts—pink trimmed with white, white with red, red with pink—are like so many giant carnations that have been tumbled upon the town. At its end the sleepless, exhausted, happy, hung-over Sevillanos must topple like dancers from a tarantella. Again the city sinks into its lethargy, to slumber and dream for another eleven months with only the tourists to stir the languid movement of life along its rather untidy streets.

Faces of Spain

From *There Is Indeed But One Ronda,* by Hamilton Basso, © 1956, The New Yorker Magazine, Inc., reprinted by permission.

Along with the ever-changing landscape, along with this face of Spain, there are the faces of the people you stop to talk with. These would be the men, mostly—farmers and shepherds and wagoners and laborers on the roads—and there is always time enough to take time out. "Command me," they say. "What is it that I can do?" Then, when you inquire about a distance or a direction or a place to stay, there is sudden collapse of the severe presence with which the Spaniard confronts the world, and you notice the quick, warm desire to establish the kind of truly human communication that is based on unfailing courtesy and pride. The raggedest vagrant or poorest countryman knows that he is your equal and the equal of any man, and, in his own secret heart, that he is perhaps a little better than most—a Christian gentleman, an old and wellborn one (*cristiano viejo y rancio*)—and he conducts himself accordingly. Whatever the offenses or iniquities of its economic structure—and they are many—Spain is in this respect a completely classless country.

Barcelona's Sacred Family Church

From *Let's Visit Spain,* copyright, 1954, by Frank E. Howell, reprinted by permission of Thomas Y. Crowell Company, the publishers.

La Sagrada Familia, designed by Antonio Gaudi, although not finished, is probably the most unusual piece of architecture in Spain. Like "Mystic Poem Worked in Stone" it was started by F. del Vilar in 1882, the great Catalan architect Gaudi taking over in 1884. He used his own radical ideas and the result is amazing. If he had lived, we feel sure he would have completed an architectural gem of original style different from anything yet attempted in any part of the world, and all of it with a meaning, an expression, as it were, of spiritual inspiration. He has worked in, for example, representations of biblical scenes, the Apostles, children, animals, flowers, fruits, trees, musical instruments, angels and many other figures all blended by the natural color of the stone. The lower part of the building is today used for Mass. A visit will give one the idea of how beautiful the main chapel would have been—or will be when completed.

The Mountain Monastery of Montserrat

From *Introducing Spain,* copyright, 1956, by Cedric Salter, reprinted by permission of William Sloane Associates, Inc., and Methuen & Co., Ltd.

No. 1 sight-seeing excursion from Barcelona is undoubtedly that to the mountain monastery of Montserrat, some 30 miles inland from the city, with a chance to do the last 2½ miles by aerial railway, which is exciting but safe. This strange serrated peak, towering dramatically out of the Llobregat plain, is so rich in legend that even though it can be visited by charabanc it has somehow still managed to preserve a certain kind of Shangri-la atmosphere of mystery. It is the setting, far more than the buildings, that is remarkable, with huge petrified fingers of rock pointing accusingly toward the sky.

If it is anything like a clear day you will see the whole snow-capped mass of the eastern Pyrenees piled up over 100 miles away on the northern horizon, even before you reach the monastery itself, which is built in a small clearing at the base of the towering stone fingers. It is only when you penetrate into the not particularly beautiful, recently restored church, and find yourself in the presence of the little Black Virgin, that you will begin to understand why this mountain has always been a place of pilgrimage. I have been to many such, including those in the Holy Land, but nowhere have I felt the same sense of power as radiates from that small, and to me slightly sinister-seeming figure. A small stairway behind the High Altar allows you to see it close, level, and face to face, and even to touch the orb that it holds in one of its hands.

Jerez, City of Sherry

From *Fabled Shore,* by Rose Macaulay, reprinted by permission of Farrar, Straus and Cudahy, Inc., and Hamish Hamilton, Ltd.

Jerez, the Roman Caesaris Asidonia, the Arab Caeris Sidonia, is a most pleasant city. It has been called white; but it seemed to me to be for the most part sherry colored. The palacios, the churches, the plazas, were mostly of the local apricot sandstone, and very charming and mellow they looked in the afternoon glow. The bodegas are mainly white, very beautifully and cleanly white, with red tiled roofs and arcaded forecourts green with orange trees. They are scattered about the town; the largest bodega establishments cover several acres, and form (like that of Manuel Misa, close to the station) a whole *barrio* of white walls, roofed and pillared arcades opening on paved courts, and long white red-tiled bodegas with bright green shuttered windows and floors. Others are on the sites, or in the converted buildings, of old churches or convents. One of the largest stands on the hill of the old Moorish Alcázar (now converted into dwellings). Inside, they are cool and dim, and aromatically delicious with the smell of wine; they are divided into aisles like a church nave, and the great casks lie in them, tier above tier, full of sherry of all dates, all colors, from rich brown to pale amber. One is shown round by kind hosts, and offered samples to taste; the result is very agreeable, and Jerez, when one emerges again into the sunlight, seems more than ever a pleasant, golden, sherry-colored town. Indeed, it is a very charming town, with an air of elegant opulence, fine manorial houses (like the sherry, of all dates) standing among palms and orange gardens, with coats-of-arms over their sculptured doors; some descend from the hereditary hidalgos, others were built in the prosperous nineteenth century by rich wine merchants of all nations.

The Women of Spain

From *The Spanish Temper,* copyright, 1954, by V. S. Pritchett, reprinted by permission of Alfred A. Knopf, Inc.

The women of Madrid, as they go by in their two and threes, and so rarely with a man, have a militant, formal, prim appearance. Sociable and talkative —for all Spaniards love talking for its own sake—they are trained to a double role: they display themselves, they have great personal pride; yet never for a moment do they allow their eyes to meet the eyes of a man as they walk the street. The decorum is complete and is distinctly Victorian. . . . As they walk by, carrying themselves so well, they are rather a collected, rather severe female race. For all this dominant appearance—and they clearly dominate the men by having their role in life firmly marked out and mix with the male very little socially—they have the reputation of being homely, innocent and sensual. They are passionate lovers of children: there is marriage and eight children in their eyes.

Yet in the past ten or fifteen years Spain has gone through revolutionary changes, and Spanish girls are experiencing a belated and relative emancipation.

The Wonders of Spain

From *Spain* by Sacheverell Sitwell, reprinted by permission of B. T. Batsford Ltd.

Spain has within its borders some of the most beautiful and wonderful creations of the hand of man. There is nothing left in Europe, or in the world today, that can compare with the cathedrals of Toledo and Seville, of Burgos and of Santiago. If we want to know what was meant by the forces and wealth of Christendom during the Middle Ages we have to visit these, and look on in awe and silence. They are overwhelming with their loaded shells heaped with the carvings, and tapestries, the pearls and gold and treasures of the centuries. The granite Escorial is still the eighth wonder of the world, inhabited, or formerly inhabited, by monks and kings, not a dead monument to the dead, like the Pyramid of Cheops; more awe-inspiring than ever Empire State Building or Rockefeller Institute could be. The 'red city' or 'red castle' of the Alhambra is one of the beauties of the world, hiding its courts of filigree and stalactite, its fountains and its myrtles, but the garden of the Generalife is lovelier still. There can be nothing in the world more beautiful than the cypresses, the singing or dancing waters, the roses and irises (an innovation), and the *mirador* (lovely word!) looking down upon Granada and the plain, and upon the hill of El Albaicín.

The Spanish Language

From *Don Fernando*, copyright, 1938, by W. Somerset Maugham, reprinted by permission of Doubleday & Company, Inc., the author and Messrs. Heinemann.

I think it was George Borrow who said that the Spanish language was greater than its literature. The statement is true. The language is an instrument of strength and delicacy. It has a grandeur that gives ample opportunity for oratorical effect (an opportunity the Spanish authors did not neglect) and a concreteness that enables it to be written with exquisite simplicity . . .

There are innumerable idioms in Spanish; they give the language pungency. It makes an ampler and more complicated use of the subjunctive than most modern languages and so gets into its speech a great elegance. We have pretty well lost the use of this mood in English and when we resort to it now it falls upon the ear affectedly; but it cannot, I think, be denied that it adds grace and distinction to a language. It is startling, and to anyone sensitive to such things charming, to hear a peasant in the course of conversation use with the accuracy of second nature the various forms of the subjunctive that the grammars give. Spanish has a harsher sound than Italian; it has not the euphonious monotony that makes that language something fatiguing to listen to; it has a leaping, quick vivacity that forces the attention. It has nobility and deliberation. Every letter counts; every syllable has value. I like the story they tell of Charles V: he said that German was the best language in which to address horses, French to converse with statesmen, Italian to talk to women, English to call the birds; but that Spanish was the only language in which to address kings, princes and God.

The Mosque of Cordova

From *The Face of Spain,* by Gerald Brenan, copyright, 1956, by Farrar, Straus & Cudahy, reprinted by permission of Farrar, Straus & Cudahy, Inc., and Turnstile Press.

The Mosque of Cordova is certainly the first building in Spain—the most original and the most beautiful. From the moment of entering the great court planted with orange trees, one gets a feeling of peace and harmony which is quite different from the mood of religious holiness and austerity imparted by Christian cloisters. The small reddish oranges cluster among the dark green leaves, butterflies chase one another, birds flit about and chirp, and the great marble cistern for ablutions seems to be there to say that the warmth and richness of Nature and the instinctive life of Man are also pure because they have been willed by God.

When one enters the mosque itself one is likely to suffer at first from conflicting impressions. The Renaissance choir built in the center disturbs one's view of the forest of columns; and then the double horseshoe arches, striped buff-white and brick-rose, arrest one by their strangeness and novelty. One has to visit the building several times to allow its magic to sink into one.

The Cathedral at Santiago de Compostela

From *Farewell, Spain,* copyright, 1937, by Kate O'Brien, reprinted by permission of Doubleday & Company, Inc.

I have seen many of the great English cathedrals and some of the French and German; I have seen Burgos and Toledo. I admit the ethereal suggestibility of Gothic, and the unearthly luminous effects sometimes of its interiors. I admit its power to seem afloat, to be on tiptoe, and that Santiago de Compostela—romanesque—renaissance—is very firmly planted on the ground. A heavy-weight. But in dimension, in proportion, in the relation of subsidiary buildings to the main, in its free and excellent decoration and in the almost modesty of its baroque towers and cupolas, it seems to me to say in a particularly powerful and sober idiom, its own, all that faith could possibly externalize of its ideal. It seems to me at once the most touching and most majestic of great temples. It has indeed at first sight a very royal and bejewelled look, but lived with, it suggests much more that life is heavy, that contrition and mercy are its constant necessities, that prayer must go on though ecstasy fail, that the Gate of Glory is only one way in to God's presence, and that in His house there are humbler doors.

I may be wrong by the book in my predilection for this mighty church. Certainly I am no expert to judge its merits and defects—and I may be seduced, as I have been all over Spain, by the colour of the sandstone. But here in this Cathedral and in the group of buildings which surrounds it, the seminary, the convent, the military school, the hospital—all sixteenth- and seventeenth-century structures of varying degrees of beauty, with the Plat er esque hospital the queen of them—here you have a settlement of mellowed, buff masonry, beneath a blue sky . . . the result is a rightness and nobility of which no eye could ever tire.

65

Lisbon in Summer

From *Portugal and Madeira,* by Sacheverell Sitwell, reprinted by permission of B. T. Batsford Ltd.

It would be hard, indeed, to exaggerate the beauty of Lisbon in the heat of August and early September. A city where, although the trams run, late and early, and motor traffic never ceases, you are woken by a cock crowing in some hidden backyard or corner of a garden, and standing at the window you look down at the bank of geraniums in front of the house opposite and they are glowing, in incandescence, like blind flowers, for the dawn has not reached to them; the palm trees are but shadows of themselves, and looking up over the roofs the morning just touches, that moment, on the white walls of a castle, high up, the Castelo de São Jorge, lie a celestial city in a cloudless sky. The next sound may well be the pan-pipes of the knife-grinder at the street corner, for you sleep long in Lisbon on the summer mornings, going to bed late at nights and taking a long siesta in the afternoons. Altogether, there can be no lovelier summer city than Lisbon in late August or early September. . . .

The Rossio, Nerve-center of Lisbon

From *Spain and Portugal,* edited by Doré Ogrizek, copyright in Great Britain, 1953, reprinted by permission of the McGraw-Hill Book Company, Inc.

Lisbon is still suffering from acute growing-pains and it spills over from its seven hills. But its center of gravity has not shifted and the whole city continues to revolve around the Rossio as though around some pivot. In the beginning it was a vast stretch of barren ground where they held cattle-fairs and horse-races. . . . The Rossio very soon became urban in character and it has scarcely changed. You still find fountains, cafés, flower-girls, a confused mass of vehicles, and a crowd of busy people amidst an even bigger crowd of people who have nothing to do.

The latest editions of the London and Paris newspapers, flown over, are on sale; people discuss international politics and show an equal interest in the women who pass by. Although the fine central esplanade, with its black and white mosaics, has been broken up into three sections, and although half the trees have been cut down to ease the flow of traffic, there is still a good deal of congestion, and nearly all the tramway routes have their termini there. But the sun warms the Rossio and its rays light up the background of this amphitheater like a well-focussed stage spotlight. Though the Rossio is actually limited in extent and bounded by the fronts of somewhat commonplace buildings, yet as you look at the vastness of the setting, your eyes following the lines of mansard roofs that rise up all round, it assumes its true proportions: this is the knot that holds together the dissimilar, scattered parts of the city. That is why, when the whole plan of Lisbon was redrawn after the great earthquake by the Marquis of Pombal's architects, the integrity of the Rossio was most piously respected.

Nazaré

From *Fatima: Pilgrimage to Peace,* copyright, 1954, by April Oursler Armstrong and Martin F. Armstrong, Jr., reprinted by permission of Doubleday & Company, Inc., (Hanover House).

The people of Nazaré are quite unlike their neighbors. They claim to be of pure Phoenician descent. Darker in skin, these men of the sea still fish from craft with carved prows and strange eyes painted on the bows. Back in the days when the Duke of Wellington battled Napoleon, so the story goes, a Scotch ship was wrecked on the treacherous sand bars of Nazaré Harbor. The townsfolk caught their first glimpse of a tartan. Plaid hypnotized them, but the Scotch greens and reds seemed a little prosaic to the Nazarenes. They fell to weaving their own, in pink and yellow and pale green, orange and purple, azure and coral and black. They cling to them still. The one rule of fashion on that sandy stretch of coast is that the plaid of a shirt must never match the plaid of the trousers or skirt with which it is worn. And the patches must match nothing at all.

The beach is broad and beautiful, strewn with nets drying in the sun, and fishermen coiling and knotting their ropes beside their flamboyant boats. Children skitter through the sand, browned and laughing, hiding behind pigskins full of fresh water, or under the sails stretched out for mending. Nazaré is a haven of color and joy when the fishermen are home. The harbor lies at the foot of a startling steep cliff, jagged against the cloudless sky.

Oporto, Home of "Port"

From: *Europe, A Journey With Pictures,* by Anne Fremantle and Bryan Holme, copyright, 1954, by Thomas Y. Crowell Company, reprinted by permission.

Oporto is on the Douro. This crowded commercial, industrial, and capital city of north Portugal has a large harbor with interesting and varied craft, two iron bridges (one built by Eiffel of Paris), narrow streets with traders on donkeys or in ox-driven carts mingling with the modern traffic, and exotic parks and gardens. Here aloes and citrus trees grow naturally with all the common plants and flowers of northern Europe. The neighboring vineyards too are legendary, for Oporto made its fortune with wine and gives its name to the only authentic "port" in the world. In the midst of glorious hillside scenery it is still common to find barefoot natives crushing their purple harvests—to music, furthermore, just as they have always done since anyone can remember.

Oporto has fine churches and a Cathedral, a museum, opera, and bull ring. It has memories of Wellington who drove out the French in 1809 and ate with relish the dinner that had been prepared for Napoleon's Marshal Soult, and of sedan chairs which were a common sight right up to the present century. Both these and the plaid materials still worn by the Portuguese were the result of contact with the British, who did much to develop the port industry. Besides its wine, Oporto busies itself with the fishing industry (sardines are legion), pottery, cotton, silk, leather and jewelry, rivaling Lisbon, its great competitor in the south. . . .

Portuguese Regional Cooking

From the column, *Amy Vanderbilt's Etiquette,* by Amy Vanderbilt, copyright, 1957, by United Feature Syndicate, Inc., reprinted by permission.

The Portuguese are always delighted to explain the ingredients of regional dishes, and if you wish to try them, it is probably best to start with things that have some similarity to your regular diet. Best of all in regional Portuguese cooking is the fish. Every place in Portugal is within a short distance of the sea, and fish is the main food of the people.

The main one of such dishes is codfish, Bacalhau, served in a variety of ways, dried and fresh. It usually is found delectable by foreigners. Portugal's national dish may be served in tasty little cakes, both hot and cold, in a concoction of scrambled eggs, garlic, and olive oil (not for me, but perhaps for you) and in literally a thousand and one ways. Like all the other delectable fish in Portugal, it can always be had plain, boiled with butter or grilled. The grilling is done over the hot embers of a wood fire which makes it crackling crisp. As you travel through the ever-green countryside of Portugal, you will find little signs on the buildings and in restaurant windows reading "Ha Leitão." This means that suckling pig, always considered a great delicacy, is available. The skin is very crisp. And it is served with lots of garlic, so whether or not you eat it depends on your taste for garlic.

Green Fields and Green Mountains in Minho

From *Portugal,* by Dr. George Kish, copyright ©, 1957, by Nelson Doubleday, Inc., reprinted by permission of the publisher.

The province of Minho, the northernmost part of Portugal, takes its name from the river that has its source in nearby Spain and whose winding valley is the Spanish-Portuguese frontier. Like the other regions facing the Atlantic, Minho too has a coastal area of steep, rocky shores, and a mountainous interior. The climate here is cool, rainy, and resembles western France and southern England much more than the warm, dry lands of central and southern Portugal. The winters are cold, and there is occasionally heavy snow on the mountains in the interior.

It is in the spring that the Minho countryside is at its loveliest. It is a symphony of green, the brilliant green of young corn, the light green of meadows that are bordered by fruit trees intertwined with grapevines, the soft silvery green of olives, the dark green of pines on the mountainsides. Corn is more important here than wheat, and corn meal is a popular dish. Most farms have a small orchard and a vineyard, and the farmers make their own light dry wine every year. The rivers are rich in trout and in salmon that come from the Atlantic to spawn here, and a meal even in a small country inn is likely to provide a varied menu of fish and roast, of tender greens, and, in the fall, excellent peaches and apples.

The Orchard of Portugal

From *Fabled Shore,* by Rose Macaulay, reprinted by permission of Farrar, Straus and Cudahy, Inc., and Hamish Hamilton, Ltd.

It was cool in Portugal; much cooler than it had been in Spain. My road ran delightfully between white walls and cactus hedges in golden flower. The houses were small and white, with doors and windows painted deep blue. Fig trees, olives, carobs, aloes, almonds, pomegranates, melons, oranges and lemons, all the fruits imaginable, grew in groves along the way. For this was Algarve, the orchard of Portugal. It is, I know, often hot in Algarve in summer; on this end-of-August afternoon it was coolish, with a breeze blowing in from the Atlantic. It was different from Spain—gentler, softer, less vivid. The people were different, less handsome, smaller and squatter, with faces more round and undefined, more of the Negro, less of the Moor (even though Algarve was for over five hundred years a Moorish kingdom).

Many of the women wore men's bowler hats, tied under the chin with scarves; there were straw hats everywhere; men and women rode on donkeys with umbrellas up against the sun. There was the endearing Portuguese nasal twang. It was charming to be in Portugal again. I came to Tavira, the Roman Balsa, once Algarve's capital, lying beautifully on either side of the river Gilão, or Sequa, with its ancient bridge. A delightful Moorish town, with palmy arcaded praça and white houses. The church of Santa Maria do Castelo, once a mosque, is thirteenth century; it has the tomb of that Correa who won Tavira from the Moors in 1242, and of seven knights slain by Moors while hunting. The sixteenth-century church of the Misericordia has a fine Renaissance door and manueline windows. Having briefly admired these and other charming details, I drove on along the coast road.

On the following double-page spread is a photograph of the tiny Principality of Monaco, on the Mediterranean, celebrated for its gaming casinos and postage stamps.

© PAA

Monte Carlo in the Principality of Monaco

This country is only 370 acres in area, less than half the size of New York's Central Park, or about the size of a typical Kansas farm. It is ruled by a hereditary prince and has been for the last 650 years and he is its thirty-first ruler. Monte Carlo's citizens, though by no means poor, pay no income tax because they don't have to. They traditionally haven't paid income tax and presumably won't for many years to come because of the presence in their country of a foreigner from Philadelphia, one Grace Patricia Kelly, who next to Margaret of England is the most celebrated princess of our day. The reason that citizens of Monte Carlo pay no income tax is that the monies left behind by the tourists—Monte Carlo's sole industry—easily pay the expenses of running the country. Nor are residents of Monte Carlo subject to conscription by the French army (France "rules" Monte Carlo by treaty), and the fact that this condition will continue is a result of the birth of Princess Caroline to Princess Grace and Prince Rainier in 1957. Had their been no heir to the Monacan throne, the country would have fallen under direct French rule, an income tax would have been imposed and conscription put into effect.

This country's most striking vegetation is its palm trees, of which it has exactly 498; summer and winter they wave murmurously beside a blindingly blue sea and a rocky, tortured coastline. This country is beautiful, heavily romantic and as fragrant as a perfume counter. The correct name of its most celebrated town is Mount Charles—in English. But for eighty years the world has known the town and the whole country as Monte Carlo. Even that is an error. The name of the country is Monaco, or more correctly, the Principality of Monaco. Monte Carlo is merely one of the three villages of Monaco, a country on the Mediterranean about halfway between Nice and the Italian-French border.

The Veterans

We hung around the *cuisine* for quite a while before we played. This was the serious time of day—there were no tourists and the *Salle Privée* was closed and only the veterans sat there. You had a feeling with all of them that their lunch depended on victory. It was long, hard, dull employment for them—a cup of coffee and then to work till lunchtime—if their system was successful and they could afford the lunch. Once Cary laughed—I forget what at—and an old man and an old woman raised their heads from opposite sides of the table and stonily stared. They were offended by our frivolity: this was no game to them. Even if the system worked, what a toil went into earning the 2500 francs a week. With their pads and their charts they left nothing to chance, and yet over and over again chance nipped in and shoveled away their tokens.

Gambling Sixteen Hours a Day

From *The French Riviera*, by Tom and Jean Hollyman, in *Holiday*, copyright, 1948, by The Curtis Publishing Company, reprinted by permission.

The Monte Carlo gambling syndicate, which operates in Monaco, supports the government with a tidy cut of its profits. The Casino, started in 1858, has consistently made money simply because the gambling odds are mathematically tilted in favor of the house. Roulette is still the Casino's big game, although the card games of Baccarat and *trente et quarante* are popular. Minimum bet in the Casino is about six cents and the maximum about $200, not counting the slot machines which operate for small sums in the foyer.

Each morning before the Casino's sixteen-hour day begins, the wheels are checked with a spirit balance, and clean diamond-shaped patches are sewed on the tables. Meanwhile the cashier of the "bank" of Monte Carlo and his assistants are counting money and chips for the day's play. A few of the staff of 350 croupiers appear and lay the chips out at their respective tables and await the appearance of the first gamblers. Gone for the most part are the system players who in the old days lined up mornings outside the Casino to get first crack at a "hot" number which their mathematics or tea leaves has convinced them was bound to turn up. The drab Victorian decorations inside the Casino and the grim attitudes with which the customers gamble today make the place look more like a family bank than a palace of pleasure. . . . Luckless players can always get help from the pawnshops in Monte Carlo; most of the better shops have emergency bells for customers who need after-hours aid. The little kingdom thinks of the tourist's every need.

On the following double-page spread is a photograph of Venice's Grand Canal, one of the most romantic waterways in the world. It is 2 miles long, approximately 228 feet wide.

KRONFELD © PAA

Venice

From *Venice Observed,* by Mary McCarthy, published by Reynal & Company, Inc., reprinted by permission of the publisher.

It is all for the ear and eye, this city, but primarily for the eye. Built on water, it is an endless succession of reflections and echoes, a mirroring. . . . And no word can be spoken in this city that is not an echo of something said before. *"Mais c'est aussi cher que Paris!"* exclaims a Frenchman in a restaurant, unaware that he repeats Montaigne. . . .

Nothing can be said here (including this statement) *that has not been said before.* One often hears the piazza described as an open air-drawing-room; the observation goes back to Napoleon, who called it "the best drawing room in Europe." A friend likens the ornamental coping of St. Mark's to sea foam, but Ruskin thought of this first: " . . . at last, as if in ecstasy, the crests of the arches break into a marble foam, and toss themselves far into the blue sky in flashes and wreaths of sculptured spray . . ." Another friend observes that the gondolas are like hearses; I was struck by the novelty of the fancy until I found it, two days later, in Shelley: "that funereal bark." Now I find it everywhere. A young man, boarding the vaporetto, sighs that "Venice is so urban," a remark which at least *sounds* original and doubtless did when Proust spoke of the "always urban impression" made by Venice in the midst of the sea. And the worst of it is that nearly all these clichés are true. It is true, for example, that St. Mark's at night looks like a painted stage flat; this is a fact which everybody thinks he has discovered for himself. I blush to remember the sound of my own voice, clear in its own conceit, enunciating this proposition in the Piazza, nine years ago. One accepts the fact that what one is about to feel and say has not only been said before by Goethe or Musset but is on the tip of the tongue of the tourist from Iowa who is alighting in the Piazzatta with his wife in her furpiece and jeweled pin.

The Beauty of the Italian Lakes

From *European Journey,* copyright, 1934, by Philip Gibbs, reprinted by permission of Curtis Brown, Ltd., London.

Baveno is a neat and pleasant little town on the edge of the Lago di Maggiore, where the beauty of Italy is like a dream of Paradise. There are other lovely places in the world—so many!—not yet spoiled by the ugly touch of modern "progress"; but around these Italian lakes beauty is almost too enchanting. One is aware of a langor overcoming one's spirit. The hustle and bustle of modern life seems so foolish and unnecessary. It is difficult to be active and aggressive. One sinks into lethargy, and the spirit of *dolce far niente* would weaken the urge of a profiteer to make more profit by calling down his telephone, when, here, beauty offers all the wealth of life to be drunk in by the eye, to enter into the pores of one's skin, to make one a sun worshipper, to put a spell upon one's senses. On the Italian lakes . . . it needs terrific will power to address a picture postcard to one's nearest and dearest.

Rome from the Air

In the air, from which you get no idea of any "seven hills" (the number in any case has been juggled considerably: one hill consists entirely of ancient potsherds, another was carted away to make room for an emperor's forum, three of the original seven are now humped together as one) but you do see a few ups and downs, and the mountains high all around, beautifully streaked with snow in winter, of which you will always be conscious later as of the sea and its ship sounds around Manhattan; you see them from any rise, and along the Tiber, and down at the end of many long streets, as if it were a backdrop in a photographer's booth. They give the city a transitory look, these mountains; it seems that it could have grown up anywhere among them, or could be moved quite easily, but that is counteracted a little by the broken lines of the old aqueducts, not romantic at all from up there, coming in across the flat country; coming in much farther than you would ever think from below, to blend with sections of the brick Aurelian wall right in the busiest tangle of the city. They are of course distinctly Roman, so are the eccentric course and color of the Tiber, and the fury of the little figures you see twitching about on the football (soccer) fields, but nothing is nearly as lovely or permanent-looking in this view as the railroad tracks: a cool graph of somewhat insane lines with their ends, in a sudden reversion to control, all coming sidelong together like a boxful of pencils.

The Colosseum

The Colosseum can be seen from three or four wholly different points of view. The finest perhaps is that which is offered to the spectator when he is in the arena where the gladiators fought, and he sees those immense ruins rise all about him. What impresses me most about it is that pure blue sky that one perceives through the upper openings of the building toward the north. . . .

You see an oval theatre, of enormous height, still entire on the exterior on the north side, but ruined toward the south. It could hold 107,000 spectators.

The outer façade describes an immense ellipse; it is decorated by four orders of architecture: the two upper stories are formed of Corinthian half-columns and pilasters; the order of the ground level is Doric, and that of the second story is Ionic. The three first orders are defined by columns half sunk in the wall. . . . The world has seen nothing so magnificent as this monument; its total height is 157 feet, and its outer circumference 1641 feet. The arena where the gladiators fought is 285 feet in length by 182 in width. On the occasion of the dedication of the Colosseum by Titus, the Roman people had the pleasure of seeing five thousand lions, tigers and other wild animals put to death, as well as nearly three thousand gladiators. The games lasted one hundred days.

Roman By-ways

From *Rome,* by John Ciardi, copyright ©, 1957, by Saturday Review, Inc., reprinted by permission of the publisher.

Rome is not a planned city, as is Paris. Paris is vistas, the effect is large scale, and though one will obviously miss much in seeing it by car he will still see enough to feel rewarded. Rome on the other hand is a haphazard maze with many of its real rewards hidden around obscure corners; a façade between two nothings, or a fountain tucked away behind the pushcarts, or a gate or a ruined fragment of a courtyard come upon unexpectedly, or a medieval brick tenement wall in which one can see, trapped in the brick, the columns and a piece of the pediment of a usurped temple, or an obelisk, or a statue group, or such a wonder as Piazza Navona—all suddenly come upon just around the bend from nowhere. . . .

Above all, don't ignore the alleys. Plunge into the maze wherever you find an opening and keep going. It is never too far to a main avenue from which you can get your bearings again, and day or night you are perfectly safe in the darkest corner. . . . Don't—especially—pass up the mazes between Piazza Navona and the Pantheon, those of Trastevere, nor those behind the Teatro di Marcello. You will want days for wandering the parks of Villa Borghese, the elegance along Via Veneto, the shops along the Corso, and more days (and nights) for the Capitoline.

Light in the Eternal City

From *Roman Fountain,* copyright, 1940, by Hugh Walpole, reprinted by permission of Doubleday & Company, Inc.

Roman light has, it seems to me, a different quality from light in any other place. The light in Africa is clear, without mercy, so powerful that you too feel powerful. The dim light of an English spring day is germinating light, rich with seed, promising flowers through rain. The light of Russia pouring down upon steel-silver snow is ancient and boundless. The light of Egypt, as you wake in early morning on the Nile, is fresher than any other in the world, and is like the *beginning* of the world. The light in California is seasonless and thin, but eternal. It seems there impossible that it should ever be dark. . . . During the spring and the autumn Roman light has a life of its own, as though, in the sky, there were an activity quite independent of the earth. When you are on one of the Roman hills you seem to be in a world of light that is neither the world of the earth nor the world of the heavens above, and, from the Janiculum, I have seen Rome soaked in a light that removes it both from earth and sky. Florence and Venice, the two other most beautiful towns in the world, are often unreal because of their beauty, but they live in *one* light which is a miracle but a reasonable miracle. The Roman light gives you three worlds, and the best of these is the one that you never see but know to be there.

The Trevi Fountain

From *Rome: Fragments in the Sun,* by Laurence Scarfe, reprinted by permission of Roy Publishers.

This fountain is the most grandiose baroque monument in Rome, built in thirty years in the mid-eighteenth century. Against the severe and heavy background of the Palazzo Poli, Neptune stands in a great nautilus shell drawn by two ramping sea horses led by tritons. Over a rockery, with many subsidiary rills and spouts, cascades of water rush into the huge basin beneath. In front of the fountain are wide and ample steps and benches, on which the people of the neighborhood gather.

The Trevi Fountain has a special attraction for young boys, who, dodging the not too watchful eyes of the policemen, wade in to look for the coins thrown in by visitors who wish to return to Rome. There is many an exciting chase if they become too much of a nuisance. Amid roars of laughter from the idling people, a small boy will scramble up over the rocks, behind the seahorses, down at the other side, and disappear up a side street. The policeman, of course, hasn't a chance, but plays the little comedy out, time and again, as part of his duties.

At any time the Trevi Fountain is a lovely sight, but at night it is transformed into a stage set, lit by the street lamps and the glow from the shops. The grey and white stone is contrasted with the surrounding houses painted red and ochre, and every evening there is a spontaneous aquatic carnival in which the citizens take part, enlivened by rushing water and the dancing reflections.

The Borghese Gardens

From *Europe Without Baedeker,* copyright, 1947, by Edmund Wilson, reprinted by permission of the author.

The Borghese Gardens—into which you pass, are at the top of the broad Via Veneto, through the old chipped reddish weedy Roman wall and the stone gates with the modern eagles. Here one always finds an atmosphere of gaiety, of leafage, of light bright color—everything both larger and more casual than in a park in London or Paris, and enchanting with a freedom and felicity that are characteristic only of Rome—all a little not precisely tinselly, not precisely flimsy, but slightly both tempting and teasing the foreigner by a careless disregard of plan, a cheerful indifference to purpose, that, nevertheless, acquire a certain insolence from blooming among the monuments of so much solid civic building, so much noble and luxurious beauty.

I found myself almost every afternoon, when I had been to call for my mail, wandering up into the Borghese Gardens to read it and the Italian papers in a little out-of-doors café called La Casina del Lago. You went inside a special enclosure, shut off from the rest of the park by a little black iron fence, behind which were posted at intervals, whitish and dim in the shadow, a set of small antique statues, and walked along a gravelled alley vaulted with fine straight green oaks, which seemed marvellously cool and reposeful after the dirty main drive and the meridian heat.

The Spanish Steps

From *Rome of the Renaissance and Today,* by Sir James Rennell Rodd, G.C.B., published by Macmillan and Co., Limited, London, reprinted by permission of the publisher.

Whether you first enter the Spanish Piazza, as travelers did in the old coaching days, from the northern end of its irregular parallelogram, or from the southern end, as the visitor of today has more often occasion to do, or from the Via de' Condotti which links it with the Corso, your eye will inevitably be arrested and enchanted by the noble which ascends the slope of the "Hill of Gardens." On the summit is a golden church with double towers known as the Trinita de' Monti, which Charles VIII of France founded in memory of his sojourn in Rome in 1495. This splendid approach, with its hundred and thirty-seven steps mounting in successive flights and dividing to skirt either side of spacious platforms, was due to the munificence of a French Ambassador, M. Gouffier, whose name should be held in honor. . . . Old engravings show the church on the crest of a hill with an avenue of small trees descending to the piazza. Since the early nineties of the last century flower vendors have been allowed to erect their stalls at the base of the staircase, and these give a vivid note of color to the background of travertine tempered by time. . . .

At the foot of the steps is the fountain in the form of a ship, designed by the elder Bernini, where the water of the Aqua Virgo as it splashes over the bulwarks gives a pleasant sense of coolness in hot summer days.

Piazza della Signoria, Florence

From *Florence,* by Edward Hutton, reprinted by permission of David McKay Company, Inc., and Hollis & Carter, Ltd., London.

In every ancient city there is one spot, holy or splendid, that instantly evokes an image of that of which it is a symbol. If you name the Acropolis all the beauty and courage of Athens stirs in your heart; when you utter the word Capitolium you seem to hear the thunder of the Legions, to understand the dominion and majesty of Rome. Something of this too may still be found in the Piazza della Signoria of Florence: all the love and pride that built the city, the beauty that gave it fame, the immense confusion that is its history, linger yet in that ancient piazza which was the Forum of the Roman city, where the Ghibelline Uberti had their homes, where the Ciompi rose against them and where the Duke of Athens was expelled from the city; where Jesus Christ was proclaimed King of the Florentines, where Savonarola was burnt and Alessandro de'Medici made himself Duke. The Piazza della Signoria is the symbol of Florence—a beautiful symbol.

In the morning the piazza is full of sunlight and crowded with people. There is a cafe with a *terrazza,* there a stall for newspapers; here a lemonade merchant dispenses his drinks. Everyone is talking; at the corner of the Via Calzaiuoli a crowd assembles, a crowd that moves and seems about to dissolve, that constantly re-forms itself without ever breaking up. On the benches of the loggia in the shadow men lie asleep and children chase one another among the statues.

Taormina at Dusk

From *Easter in Sicily*, copyright, 1956, by Herbert Kubly, reprinted by permission of Simon and Schuster, Inc.

During the ride to Taormina a storm blew up as fierce as the one a week before in Syracuse. It lashed against the bus and uprooted trees in our path. Several times men passengers joined together to heave branches of oak or locust out of the road. Our progress was slow, and before we were halfway there night had fallen. In the village of Mascali we were delayed an hour by the debris in the street. . . .

The road was cleared; our bus was ready to move on. In a half hour we were at the seaside town of Giardino, where we started the long, winding climb to Taormina. I heard a rumbling which I took to be thunder but which turned out to be Etna stirring. . . . The sky over the volcano became red, and streaks of flame bombs lit up the heavens above Pluto's fiery portals of the underworld. On a ledge over Taormina a white cross of stone shone in the night; otherwise it was dark. The wild wind shrieked like Vulcan's bellows as we registered at a hotel called the Mediterraneo. I had the strange sensation of being very close to both Heaven and Hell.

Palermo—The Happy City

From *Festivals and Folkways of Italy*, by Frances Toor, copyright, 1953, by Crown Publishers, Inc., reprinted by permission of the publishers.

That gay, sunny Christmas day in Palermo, capital of Sicily, the main street was filled with well-dressed, good-looking people, chatting and laughing. They were out for their noon *passeggiata,* the married and engaged promenading in couples, young girls and young men in separate groups, furtively flirting. Many stopped at bars to eat cake and drink coffee or sweet liqueurs. My Italian friends assured me sweets before meals do not spoil the appetite. They did mine, but the delicious Sicilian pastry is hard to resist.

Christmas in Italy is not especially a time for exchanging gifts. People go to church, eat together, pay visits and send flowers. Sidewalk stands glowed with many blooms. Violets were conspicuous, for they are the language of love and young men send them to their fiancées. The festive spirit begins well before Christmas and lingers on for weeks afterwards. Peasants come down from the hills during each of the nine mornings of the Novena (December 16–24) with their primitive bagpipes to play tender little tunes to the Madonnas, in homes, stores and on street altars, for which they receive gifts of food and money. And for weeks after the midnight mass on Christmas Eve, when the Bambino Gesu is received with joyful blowing of little whistles and ringing of church bells, the public continues to pay devout homage to his image in the *presepio* or manger.

Immortal Athens

From *Greece,* by Nicholas P. Karalekas, copyright ©, 1957, by Nelson Doubleday, Inc., reprinted by permission.

For more than a thousand years Athens was the unquestioned cultural center of the Western world, but for many centuries thereafter it was nothing but a small market town of a few thousands. Today it is the strenuous, noisy, national capital of Greece, a city of almost one million inhabitants. It lies in a valley a few miles inland from the port of Piraeus, itself a big industrial city of half a million, the second largest in Greece.

Within Athens and commanding a fine view of it are two hills: Mount Lycabettos, topped by the white chapel of Saint George; and the Acropolis, meaning the height of the city, a rock plateau, on which stands the famous Temple of Athena, or Parthenon. Imposing and soul-stirring even in ruins, the Parthenon occupies the central part of the Acropolis and towers above all its neighbors. Erected under the direction of that excellent statesman, Pericles, it excelled all other buildings of ancient Athens in brilliancy of color, majesty of line, and beauty of form. It apparently opened for public worship in 438 B.C. when Phidias' statue of the goddess Athena, thirty-nine feet high, was unveiled during a festival. At night the Parthenon is floodlit and appears suspended in mid-air, a superb, glowing architectural gem.

Streets of Athens

From *Athenian Adventure,* copyright ©, 1957, by C. P. Lee, reprinted by permission of Alfred A. Knopf, Inc.

Though Athens is more chromatic than a provincial Greek town, its prevailing color is white, and the subdominant color is blue, that Greek blue a little deeper than the Greek sky and a little lighter than the Greek sea, a color used as trim on houses, on cars, on clothes. . . . Except for Plaka, on the slopes of the Acropolis, the streets are straight and cross each other at right angles, but geography has defeated a perfect gridiron pattern, for Athens, or the major part of the city, lies in a valley between two peaks, the Acropolis and Mount Lycabettus. The streets are narrow, with minute sidewalks, except for three wide avenues which curve gently from the political and tourist center of the city, Syntagma Square, flanked by the Parliament Building and the luxury hotels, to Ommonia Square, region of honky-tonks and cheap hotels. On the map these avenues bear the names of politicians: Churchill, Venizelou, and Franklin D. Roosevelt, but in popular parlance they retain older names, Stadium, University (Panepostimou), and Academia streets. . . . Although the map still retains Churchill Street, this name no longer legally exists; during the Cyprus agitation in 1955 the Churchill plaques were torn down by the mob, and the city, accepting a *fait accompli,* ceremoniously restored the old name. All streets bearing politicians' names, and there are many, retain their older names in popular speech, for the Greek realizes the motive for naming thus, and realizes, too, the justice of La Rochefoucauld's remark that gratitude is a lively sense of favors to come.

A View from the Acropolis

From *The Alps, The Danube, and The Near East,* by Frank G. Carpenter, copyright, 1924, by Carpenter's World Travels, reprinted by permission of Frances Carpenter Huntington and Doubleday & Company, Inc.

Athens is partly on and partly off the site of the ancient city. It is on the edge of a plain with the Acropolis rising upward sheer two hundred feet at its back and the low mountain of Hymettus at one side. Near this are other mountains and across the plain are the blue waters of the Mediterranean. From the Acropolis one can see the plains of Marathon where the Greeks under Miltiades defeated the Persian hosts, and away to the west lies the Bay of Salamis where Xerxes, the Persian King, watched his thousand war vessels being destroyed by the Greek fleet.

Only a stone's throw from the Acropolis is Mars' Hill, which hangs out like a cliff, forming a pulpit. There stood St. Paul and declared the religion of the Unknown God, and it was there that the Court of the Areopagus tried and convicted Demosthenes for bribery. . . .

There is no better place to study old Greece than right here in Athens. One imbibes the spirit of the ancients in tramping over the hills where they lived. One sees their wonderful works in the museums, meets with their portraits in the statues, and from the ruins scattered almost everywhere rebuilds the famed structures of the past.

Greece from the Air

From *Europe Without Baedeker,* copyright, 1947, by Edmund Wilson, reprinted by permission of the author.

When you look down and see the first Greek islands, you are surprised by the difference from Italy, whose dense plantings of parched yellow fields you have so short a time before left behind. Here is paler, purer, soberer country, which seems both wild and old and quite distinct from anything farther west. The sea is absolutely smooth, sometimes violet, sometimes blue, with a softness of water-color, glistening in patches with a fine grain of silver; and the islands of all sizes in bulbous or oblong shapes—blobs and round-bottomed bottles and the contours of plump roast fowl—seem not to rise out of the water but to be plaqued on it like cuff-links on cuffs or to lie scattered like the fragments of a picture-puzzle on a table with a blue cloth cover. These islands are a dry terra-cotta—quite unlike the deep earthy clay tints to which one has been accustomed in Italy—almost the color of two well-cooked liver, and the vegetation looks like gray lichens. The marblings on the looping beaches set up a feeling of uncanny familiarity which refers itself, as one recognizes in a moment, to the patterns on the ancient Greek vases made out of this very soil. Even on the large islands and the mainland, there are visible little cultivation and few plainly cut ribbons of roads, and the country, after humanized Italy, seems grander and more mysterious. The haze of the fawn-colored foreground shades farther away into blue, where the mountains stand dim and serene. These are the "shadowy mountains" of Homer.

The Epitomy of Liubliana

From *Yugoslav Life and Landscape,* copyright, 1954, by Alec Brown, reprinted by permission of Elek Books, Ltd.

Liubliana is a miniature, a pocket city, easily encompassed on foot in one day of that sight-seeing which consists in collecting snapshots of public buildings, urban landscapes, reputed scenes of torture and execution and public statuary. But when one tries to understand it, one finds it as mysteriously rich as a late Beethovan figure. It is dangerous to, it holds one aloof like a girl who is both beautiful and very clever, but whom it is fatal to love, for once involved, one is never free again.

The miniature river Liublianchitza winds fantastically under and among public edifices and domestic dwellings of great baroque and post-baroque urbanity. The heart of it, a knot of tangled streets (into the medley of which any Slovene will with poetic disregard for the absolute meaning of *right* and *left* lovingly misdirect the stranger) suddenly emerges on the western side into a straight business thoroughfare which, near a gracious well-vegetated park, boasts one solitary skyscraper. Over all this looms the medieval castle of Golovatz, a mass of masonry of no meagre dimensions taken straight from a romantic stage setting.

Zagreb

From *Tito Lifts the Curtain: The Story of Yugoslavia Today,* by Hallam Tennyson, reprinted by permission of Rider and Company, London.

Zagreb's European façade is certainly attractive. The old episcopal town is built on a hill to the north and the more modern part is laid out in neat segments on the flat below. The old town is Renaissance in style, with narrow, sloping streets, and walls plastered a peeling fawn or flame or petunia and decked with paneled doorways, pediments and fluted columns. Here the broken line of the roofs reminds one of Florence: Italian too are the sudden vistas of the modern city which open beneath one round corners like a chinese fan, and the froth of roses above the walls of the wealthier suburbs. Below, all is orderly and Viennese. The main streets radiate from Republic Square, which forms a fine civic centre not dominated by Government like the centre of Belgrade. Trams run between box hedges, military-looking gardens invest Government buildings in the western wing of the city, and the main restaurant is called "The Hunting Horn." On my first visit the rain was unceasing and, because of the cold, I was reduced to wearing my pyjama jacket under my shirt. But on my second visit the pavements steamed and roads bubbled with heat. This time huge awnings were stretched in front of the cafés in Republic Square and Zagreb's citizens sat out on the pavement drinking Turkish coffee, thus tacitly admitting their kinship with their more Oriental compatriots—for Turkish coffee is one of the folk customs common to the whole of Yugoslavia. Yet Austria was still not forgotten, for as the citizens drank I noticed them studiously scrutinizing their newspapers; they neither talked as much as the inhabitants of Belgrade nor stared like the Macedonians.

Dubrovnik

From *Black Lamb and Grey Falcon: A Journey Through Yugoslavia*, copyright, 1940, 1941, by Rebecca West, reprinted by permission of The Viking Press, Inc.

For an ideal first visit the traveler should go into the city and find the light just faintly blue with dusk in the open space that lies inside the gate, and has for its centre the famous fountain by the fifteenth-century Neapolitan architect Onofrio de la Cava. This is a masterpiece, the size of a small chapel, a domed piece of masonry with fourteen jets of water, each leaping from a sculptured plaque set in the middle of a panel divided by two slender pilasters, into a continuous trough that runs all around the fountain: as useful as any horsetrough, and as lovely and elevating as an altar. On the two steps that raise it from the pavement there always lie some carpets with their sellers gossiping beside them. At this hour all cats are grey and all carpets are beautiful; the colors, fused by the evening, acquire richness. On one side of this square is another of the bland little churches which Dalmatians built so often and so well. . . . At this hour its golden stone gives it an air of enjoying its own private sunset, prolonged after the common one. It has a pretty and secular rose-window which might be the brooch for a bride's bosom. Beside it is a Franciscan convent, with a most definite and sensible Pietà over a late Gothic portal.

On the following double-page spread is a photograph of Istanbul's two famous mosques: Santa Sophia, left; the Blue Mosque, right.

Istanbul's Santa Sophia

From *From An Antique Land,* by Julian Huxley, reprinted by permission of Crown Publishers, Inc., and Max Parrish & Co., Ltd.

Santa Sophia both is and deserves to be the most famous building in the city. . . . Justinian's architects were men of genius who achieved that supreme task of great architecture, the enclosure of space in a harmonious pattern, in such a way that the enclosed space, far from appearing imprisoned, reveals its inherent qualities of spaciousness, and seems almost to live, through the organic way in which its separate volumes are related into a whole. The dome, supported on four noble piers in the centre of the nave, is a masterpiece. The mind of the beholder, in that act of love and unison which great art compels, ascends into its sublimity, not drawn painfully up and ever up as by the tension of even the greatest Gothic, but floating, aerial yet secure, within its bounding curve. . . .

The great galleries constitute a separate storey all round the building; their recesses, seen through a range of supporting columns, and only half explorable by the eye from below, add a sense of intricacy to the construction without detracting from its central spaciousness. The galleries were reserved for women: here the Empress Theodora sat when she attended service in her husband's masterpiece. The walls are lined with a varied revetment of marble, and there are no less than a hundred splendid columns in the interior, many of them with very beautiful capitals. The four pairs of porphyry columns in the bays at the four corners of the nave are the most magnificent; they came from that most grandiose of temples, the Temple of the Sun at Baalbek, after having first been taken to Rome by Aurelian as booty from one of his Syrian campaigns.

Byzantium the Beautiful

From *People, Places, and Books,* copyright, 1953, by Gilbert Highet, reprinted by permission of The Oxford University Press.

The city which was called Byzantium is now called Constantinople, or rather Istanbul, in modern Turkey. . . . All that most of us know about it is that it was beautiful. Its center was one of the loveliest buildings in the entire world, something worthy to rank with the Taj Mahal and Notre Dame: the Cathedral Church of the Holy Wisdom, St. Sophia, with its enormous, airy dome. Some of us who know the strange unforgettable paintings and mosaics of Byzantium: when you enter a Slavic or Greek church today, or look at an icon, what you see is Byzantine art: those tall thoughtful figures, with vast somber eyes. Connoisseurs know also that much of Byzantine art spread through the rest of Europe and the Middle East. So St. Mark's in Venice, St. Basil's cathedral in Moscow, the legendary palace of Harun al-Raschid in Baghdad—all these are Byzantine. In fact, we are told that it was the beauty of Byzantium which converted the Russians to Christianity.

Trebizond

From *The Towers of Trebizond,* ©, 1956, by Rose Macaulay, reprinted by permission of Farrar, Straus and Cudahy, and Hamish Hamilton, Ltd.

When we saw Trebizond lying there in its splendid bay, the sea in front and the hills behind, the cliffs and the ravines which held the ancient citadel, and the white Turkish town lying along the front and climbing up the hill, it was like seeing an old dream change its shape, as dreams do, becoming something else, for this did not seem the capital of the last Byzantine empire, but a picturesque Turkish port and town with a black beach littered with building materials, and small houses and mosques climbing the hill, and ugly buildings along the quay. The citadel, the ruins of the Comnenus palace, would be somewhere on one of the heights, buried in brambled thickets and trees; a great cliff, grown with tangled shrub, divided the city into two parts. Expecting the majestic, brooding ghost of a fallen empire, we saw, in a magnificent stagey setting, an untidy Turkish port. The ghost would be brooding on the woody cliffs and ravines, haunting the citadel and palace, scornfully taking no notice of the town that Trebizond now was, with the last Greeks expelled by the Father of the Turks twenty years back.

On the following double-page spread is a photograph of Hout Bay,
10 miles south of the city of Cape Town, Union of South Africa.
Cape Town has fine buildings, a superb harbor.

Cape Town and Culture

The steep narrow side streets of Cape Town delighted me. Somebody has said to me, "Durban is decadent and Jo'burg is *nouveau riche,* but you'll like Cape Town. It's the only place in the Union that has any history worth mentioning." I saw at once what was meant. Cape Town has a mellowness which it takes two or three centuries to produce. I had also been told that in Cape Town, I should meet the most interesting Europeans. By and large I was to find it true.

There is a direct ratio between culture and liberal thought. It is no accident that the oldest European settlement in Africa is also the most cultured and the least racially prejudiced. In two words it is more civilized. That was the fact that was to impress itself deeply on my mind during my last ten days in Africa—the fact that time is on the side of civilization. . . . Whatever may be said about the detribalized African, the detribalized European is a great improvement. But outside of Cape Town he seems to be still rare in the Union, or any other part of Africa that I know of, for that matter.

Johannesburg, City of Gold

Johannesburg is the biggest city in Africa, after Cairo, and by far the most important city south of the Sahara. What it reminded me of most was Houston, Texas, although Houston has no altitude and its gold is oil. In quickness of tempo, somewhat crude vitality, and brilliant aggressiveness Johannesburg is the most American of all cities in Africa. Seen from an airplane at night, it provides a spectacle almost unrivaled on the continent, with its great glowing halo of lights visible for a score of miles. It is not a very big city by European standards, but it has force. . . . This is a rowdy city, tough, raw, confident, and energetic. In Johannesburg, as I heard it put, "the frontier has come to town." The altitude gives a sparkle to blood and mind, and it has (according to a booster pamphlet) 720 more hours of sunshine than Cannes or Nice. Nobody seems to be sure for whom Johannesburg was named—history moves fast. It did not exist until the discovery of gold in 1886, and thus is younger than any of its citizens under seventy. In 1890, the city did not have a single tree. Today there are more than a hundred parks, and I have never seen a community with so many tennis courts. . . . Traffic is a problem, because Johannesburg has more than 100,000 automobiles, a terrific figure for Africa. Blocks are short, and the city was laid out that way because corner property was so valuable. It was instructive to watch Europeans sitting impatiently in automobiles interminably stalled by traffic, obviously getting ulcers minute by minute, while carefree Africans sailed and sauntered down the sidewalks. . . .

Kimberley

Kimberley is not a very small city, as such things go in South Africa, but it has the atmosphere of one. It is a company town, and most of its citizens are held together by the common history of De Beers Consolidated Mines, Ltd., the great corporation that was born in Kimberley in 1888 and is now one of the most powerful business empires on earth, thoroughly dominating the world's diamond industry. Practically everybody in town works for De Beers or has worked for De Beers. Many of the old mining families have dispersed, and quite a lot of the young people of Kimberley have branched out into work unconnected with diamonds—schoolteaching, shopkeeping, manufacturing, and so on—but most of the people know each other, and one hears the same names again and again. . . . The streets of Kimberley are broad and well paved, and lined with respectable banking houses, hotels, and shops, but they twist and turn capriciously, describing odder patterns than the streets of the oldest European cities. The Kimberley streets began as the footpaths of the mining camp, and the footpaths twisted and turned to avoid casually placed shacks, the guy ropes of tents, and other impedimenta. Kimberley residents thus have a traffic labyrinth, and they are as proud of it as Londoners are of the maze of the city. . . . Many of the buildings that housed the town's first diamond brokers still stand—squat one-story brick structures, divided into cubbyholes of offices, with small windows at which dusty, impatient diggers would line up all day to haggle over their loot. There are also corrugated-iron houses that used to be portable but are now firmly rooted to the ground. . . .

The African Leopard

Pound for pound, the African leopard is the strongest, fightingest animal on earth. His strength is fantastic. He can hang an antelope *three times* his own weight, twenty feet up in a tree. . . . If a 125-pound leopard were double in weight he could subdue the 500-pound lion, the 1500-pound buffalo; play havoc with large antelope such as eland, oran, sable, and wildebeest; drag the Nile crocodile from water by its nose; and destroy any unarmed man who dared face him.

Leopards, both black and spotted, are smarter and more vicious than lions. Once he begins a fight, the leopard battles to the death. Not so the lion, who quits when the odds are against him. . . . Leopards live everywhere in Africa; on the plains, in wooded kloofs, on mountain slopes, in brush and forest. While I was writing this book, a leopard was reported to have been killed within forty miles of Johannesburg, a city of more than 650,000 persons. Because of heavy demand for skins, particularly in America, leopards are nearing extinction in certain areas, but until Africa's last wooded section and brush-grown ravine are cleared, leopards will survive.

Market in Leopoldville

From *The African Giant*, copyright, 1955, by Stuart Cloete, reprinted by permission of Houghton, Mifflin Company.

Perhaps the most illuminating thing to see in any foreign country is the market. And the enormous native market of Leopoldville is a sight never to be forgotten. To start with, it is almost exclusively female. . . . Many of the women were beautiful once you became used to African beauty. . . . They were dressed in brilliant colors—blues, reds, greens, yellows, beautifully patterned with every conceivable design and combination, their brightness rendered more bright by the sunshine. It was like an immense flower bed that swayed, undulated. . . .

The wares exposed for sale consisted of everything the African heart could desire. Materials, scented soap, perfume, alarm clocks, beads, hardware, and food in the utmost profusion and variety. Fish from the river and the sea. . . . There was dried fish and meat. At one stall an enormous woman was cutting up chunks of smoked elephant flesh with a chopper. At the next, dried caterpillars were exposed for sale. There were piles of manioc that looked like chunks of chalk, and manioc bread wrapped in leaves and tied with raffia. There were medicine stalls where skulls, bits of animal skins, and roots and herbs were offered. There were fruits of every kind, and nuts.

Elephant School in the Congo

From *Seven Wonders of the World*, copyright ©, 1956, by Lowell Thomas and reprinted by permission of Doubleday & Company, Inc. (Hanover House)

Africa has the largest number and variety of great beasts. In Asia there are the tiger, the elephant, the rhinoceros. But Africa has the lion, leopard, elephant, rhinoceros, hippopotamus, giraffe, not counting myriads of antelope. . . . There was an old theory that the African elephant, unlike the Indian species, could not be tamed, that it was too intractable, too savage in temperament. How incorrect that was could be seen at the elephant school in the Belgian Congo, where the proceedings began with the capture of a baby elephant from a wild herd and continued with the education of the pupil. The tribesmen use trained elephants to shunt off the wild ones. You see them isolate the calf from its mother, and drive it off, while the old bull of the herd trumpets in protest. A place outside the village is the school. Tethered to stakes, the pupil is made to kneel and rise at command, and given bananas and other rewards for good performance. The baby elephant trumpets with resentment but takes the bananas with its trunk. The day of class work ends with a procession of elephants, the natives riding them singing a song. In the distance is the old bull of the herd trumpeting. This education for African pachyderms brings to mind the most remarkable affair of elephants in all annals—the story of Hannibal's elephants. In his astounding march to strike at Rome, the Carthaginian hero's army included a squadron of war elephants, and one historical question has been, Where did he get them? The consensus of historians today is that they were African elephants.

Elisabethville

From *The Heart of Africa,* copyright, 1954, by Alexander Campbell, reprinted by permission of Alfred A. Knopf, Inc.

Elisabethville has pretty streets, some of them cobbled, and is surrounded by pleasant green meadows. The houses are picturesque, with high-pointed slate roofs and red-painted doors and windows. As in other parts of the Congo, you don't get any feeling of being within a thousand miles of Africa. Elisabethville also contains the imposing offices of the CSK, the UMHK, and other giant corporations. The creation of Elisabethville was *decreed* in 1910. There was nothing there at all. Then a provincial governor said there ought to be, and there was. . . . I stopped frequently to admire the gardens, filled with tropical blooms, and the handsome statues in the town's large squares. Women, wearing shorts, were bicycling briskly about with shopping baskets attached to their handlebars. Men, in white tropical suits, were sitting at tables on the sidewalks, drinking beer.

Flying Over the Belgian Congo

From *Jambo Means Hello,* by Olle Strandberg & Rune Hassner, copyright ©, 1956, by Olof George Strandberg, reprinted by permission of Houghton Mifflin Company.

Some years before I had flown over that part of the Congo in a little sports aeroplane together with two Belgian prospectors who were looking for wolfram and uranium. It is, perhaps, the most desolate and mysterious region of Africa. The bamboo woods streaked the sides of the hills like blue-grey, pelting rain, and clouds swept along above the tree-tops of the virgin forest with an almost solid force. Far beneath the clouds and leaves and branches I knew that there lay a land of eternal twilight, filled with shadows, unknown animals and strange races of men. Here and there we could see a narrow column of smoke rising up from a place where probably no white man had yet set foot—not having had any rational reason for doing so. But now the atom age, with its thirst for radio-active substances and metals suitable for alloys for jet engines, had thrust its way into those gloomy jungles where the Stone Age still lingered —shy, hunted and doomed to die.

The road up towards the Ituri Forest—as the very heart of that land of shadows is called—is brick-red in color and as well maintained as most roads in the Belgian Congo. A good deal of the road work is performed by convicts. Those who used to be Leopard men, bullies and thieves provide a good and cheap source of labor, and we were well able to appreciate the awkwardness of the situation which had necessitated the notice we read in the bar of a pleasant and comfortable jungle hotel at which we put up one night, in which the management "regretted that owing to the prevailing shortage of convicts, the hotel garden looked so badly kept."

Women of Ghana

From *The Heart of Africa,* copyright, 1954, by Alexander Campbell, reprinted by permission of Alfred A. Knopf, Inc.

Over most of Africa women have a chattel status. They do the hard work while the men sit around smoking their pipes, drinking their beer, and discussing village politics. But in the Gold Coast [Ghana] and also in Nigeria the women were not content simply to bear children and carry headloads. They went into business. The result today is that instead of carrying headloads, they own and operate trucks. Politics are left to the men, but the women handle the cash. From such humble beginnings as buying and selling handfuls of dried peas, some of them have built up businesses worth thousands of dollars. The United Africa Company is one of the biggest and shrewdest trading concerns in the world; but, at the very doors of its stores, Gold Coast "mammies" calmly sell the same goods as it does—at cut prices. Gold Coast men do not resent the economic independence of their women. They simply grab as large a share of the profits their wives will let them have—and go on talking politics.

Accra Street Scene

From *Black Power,* copyright, 1954, by Richard Wright, reprinted by permission of Harper & Brothers.

In front of the Indian, Syrian, and European stores African women sat before wooden boxes heaped high with red peppers, oranges, plantains, cigarettes, cakes of soap cut into tiny bits, okra, tomatoes, peeled coconuts, small heaps of matches, cans of tinned milk, etc. Men from the Northern Territories, dressed in long smocks, sold from carts piled with cheap mirrors, shoestrings, flashlights, combs, nail files, talcum powder, locks, and cheaply framed photos of Hollywood movie stars. . . . I was astonished to find that even the children were engaged in this street trade, carrying their wares on their heads either in calabashes or brass pans that had been polished until they glittered. Was it a lack of capital that made the Africans sell like this on the streets? One could buy bread from a little girl who carried a big box, screened-in, upon her cranium; one could buy a concoction called *kenke*—a kind of crushed corn that had been cooked and steamed and seasoned with pepper—from a woman who balanced an enormous, steaming calabash upon her head; one could buy baby bonnets from a woman who had layers of them stored in a brass pan that was borne aloft; yet another woman sold soap from a stack which held at least forty cakes perched atop her skull; one could buy lengths of colored cloth from a woman the top of whose head was a small dry-goods store; one could buy fish, eggs, chickens, meat, yams, bananas, salt, sugar, plantains, cigarettes, ink, pens, pencils, paper—and all of this was but "one flight up," that is, above the heads of the street women who were popularly known as "mammies."

An Ancient Art in Liberia

From *New Song in a Strange Land,* copyright, 1948, by Esther S. Warner and Gerald Dendel, reprinted by permission of Houghton Mifflin Company.

I sat on the mat and watched. The smith brushed the figure with wet clay. As soon as this first clay layer had dried, another was added, then another, until the wax was a core in a thick lump of mud. An opening was left from one of the figure's feet to the outside of the clay. Another smaller opening was made from the head to the exterior of the mud mold.

Quay-Quay worked the bellows. They were pouches of monkey skin attached to a hollow mound of clay. By punching one skin and then the other, air was forced through the mound of clay and out a small opening on the opposite side where charcoal burned. Thus were the brass shavings melted after long exertion at the bellows. When the brass was molten, it was carefully poured into the opening in the foot end of the mold. As the wax melted, it ran out the head end, the metal taking its place in the mold. "The wax, he lost proper, now," the smith said, as a fine thread of metal trickled out the head end.

When the brass had cooled and the clay was removed, the little fertility god was technically perfect. The bump of its head where the brass had trickled down the vent left for the melted wax was filed away. It was ready for whatever use Quay-Quay could make of it. The lost-wax process was not lost. Here was the *cire-perdue* process used by Greek sculptors four hundred years before Christ. How did the technique find its way into the Liberian forests? The answer may lie in the Benin bronzes. (Some authorities believe that the Portuguese brought a knowledge of *cire-perdue* to Benin.) Here in the jungle where so few things survive for any length of time, an old art still lived.

Liberia, Proud of Its Independence

From *Introducing Africa,* copyright, 1954, by Carveth Wells, reprinted by permission of G. P. Putnam's Sons.

On May 27, 1943, Edwin Barclay, grandson of American slaves, President of the Liberian Republic, became the first Negro in history to appear before the United States Congress and be officially introduced from its rostrums. The chief executive of this little West African country, founded in 1822 by American freedmen, was repaying the call which President Roosevelt made to Liberia after his conference in Casablanca with Prime Minister Churchill. About the same size as Ohio, Liberia stretches along the coast for three hundred miles from Sierra Leone to Cape Palmas, around which ships must sail when they enter the Gulf of Guinea.

Its government is to a great degree dependent economically upon the Firestone Rubber Company and politically upon the protection of the United States of America.

97

Modern Cairo

From *In Search of a Future,* copyright, 1949, by Maurice Hindus, reprinted by permission of Doubleday & Company, Inc., and the author.

A place of startling contrasts and sensational incongruities, Cairo is one of the oldest cities in the world. Founded presumably by Babylonian mercenaries in 525 B. C., it has witnessed a fabulous rise in the twentieth century.

Visitors to the Egyptian capital cannot help marveling at the energy and imagination which have gone into building so magnificent a city on the edge of a dreary sand-blown desert. Here is the East, at its best and at its worst, and the West, too, at its best but mostly at its worst. The neon lights are as resplendent as those of any city in the world, yet the kerosene lamp, often empty because there is no money to buy the oil, is as cherished as the mud-brick oven. Hotels, night clubs, other gay resorts, are as bright with light as those in any Western city, but only one fourth of Cairo's population has electric lights at home. Thanks principally to British enterprise, Cairo, unlike other cities in the Moslem Middle East, has underground installations for water and sewage. Yet, except in the select hotels and restaurants, it is unsafe to eat raw fruits, vegetables, or salads, or to drink raw milk. "Gyppy tummy" and virulent fever of one kind or another may lie in ambush in the gleaming fruit and succulent leaves served the foreigner. The richest and most cultivated Moslem city in the world, Cairo is also the citadel of Mohammedan orthodoxy—the home of the far-famed University Mosque of el-Azhar. Founded in 972, it now has an enrollment of over thirteen thousand, of whom six hundred are Moslem students from all over the world.

Climbing a Matterhorn of Masonry

From *Burton Holmes Travelogues,* copyright, 1910, by E. Burton Holmes, reprinted by permission.

You cannot conceive of the immensity of the Great Pyramid until you have been boosted up and then been hauled down the northern slope of this stone mountain made with hands—this Matterhorn of masonry, this one surviving wonder of the Seven Wonders of the World. The steps are narrow, barely fifteen inches wide; and to make matters worse for us, these steps are very high, about three feet. Each step is just a trifle higher than the average leg and knee can manage. Hence the prosperity of that wild tribe of pyramid Araba, the white-robed haulers and boosters who chaperon the traveler up and down for a fixed fee and all the *backsheesh* they can wheedle out of him. Climbing Cheops marks one of the big moments in the life of a traveler. That moment has now come for us. No wonder that we wear a look of tired triumph as we stand for the first time upon this artificial mountain-peak, older than many of the real mountains of the world. From the top of the Great Pyramid of Cheops, which, owing to the removal of the blocks that formed the apex, is now a level platform some thirty-six feet square, we look down upon the Second Pyramid, the tomb of King Kephren. . . .

Luxor

From *Any Old Place With You,* copyright ©, 1957, by William K. Zinsser, reprinted by permission of Simon and Schuster, Inc.

Luxor is probably the most bewitching site of antiquity. I had been there once before, and over the years it kept tugging me back. Luxor itself is not old. It is a shabby Arab town that has grown up over the ruins of ancient Thebes, the capital of the vast Middle Kingdom empire. In its main square are the immense columns of the temple of Amenhotep III. Two miles away is the peerless temple of Karnak, and across the Nile—in the Valley of the Dead—are the tombs where a royal line of pharaohs buried themselves with enough gold to last several lifetimes. . . .

The next day Ali took us around the temples of Karnak and Luxor. There is something hypnotic about the lordly columns and graceful wall paintings, the lovely statues, obelisks and avenues of sphinxes built to honor ancient gods. By the end of the day we were steeped in the atmosphere of the kingdom that flourished twenty centuries before Christ.

The Sphinx

From *Cairo to Kisumu,* copyright, 1923, by Frank G. Carpenter, reprinted by permission of Frances Carpenter Huntington and Doubleday & Company, Inc.

The Sphinx seems bigger, more sombre, and more wonderful than ever. Her face is that of a remarkably good-looking Negro girl, though it is said that her complexion was originally of a beautiful pink. All of this pink has now been worn away by the sands of the desert, which have for more than six thousand years been showering their amorous kisses upon it, until all that is left is a little red paint just under the left eye. That figure with the head and bust of a woman upon the body of a lion, carved out of the ages-old rock which stood here upon the desert, has been noted among the peoples of the world as far back as history extends, and those stony eyes have seen civilization after civilization rise and fall.

It would take a good-sized city lot to hold the Sphinx. The body is one hundred and forty feet long, and the paws each measure fifty feet. Her head alone is so big that a vault fourteen feet square and the height of a three-story house would be just large enough to contain it. Though you measure six feet in your stockings and have arms as long as those of Abraham Lincoln, if you stood on the tip of this old lady's ear you could hardly touch the crown of her head. The ear by actual measurement has a length of over four feet, and if that mouth would open it could swallow an ox. The nose is five feet seven inches long, and originally partook of an Ethiopian character. Now, however, it is sadly mutilated, for it has formed a target both for the conquering Mohammedans of the past and the vandal Bedouins of a later day. Tradition says, too, that Napoleon cut off the nose to spite Egypt when he was forced to retreat from the country.

The Nile

From *Egypt, Architecture, Sculpture, Painting,* by K. Lange and M. Hirmer. Translated from the German by R. H. Boothroyd, reprinted by permission of Phaidon Press, Ltd., and Hirmer Verlag.

In the well-known words of Herodotus, who traversed it about 445 B.C., the long valley of Egypt is a gift of the Nile. This mighty stream, in its 4000-mile course through half of Africa, gradually dug the valley out of the gravel-strewn desert plateau of north-eastern Africa, filling it year by year at the same season with rich, bluish-grey mud. . . .

The river, that slow-flowing, long-revered giver of life, whose course, like that of no other stream, is woven about with the glamour of legend. The sight of it awakens thoughts and impressions of a peculiar kind. These waters coming from the tropical interior of the dark continent have glided over the backs of hippopotami and over the armour-plates of crocodiles; lions have drunk of them; up in the Sudan wiry, naked black hunters have piloted their reed canoes along the gentle stream of the young Nile. Curious outlines arise before the eyes of those endowed with a feeling for the history: the god-kings of Pharaonic times are joined by the fascinating figures of an Alexander, a Caesar, an Antony, of the immortal Cleopatra whose memory lives on in the realm of dreaming fantasy, by the figures of the cooly daring conquerer Octavian, of Hadrian, and finally the silhouette of Napoleon. All of them have left indelible traces of their lives on the soil of this ancient land of wonders.

The Pied Kingfisher at Work

From *Egyptian Years,* by L. A. Tregenza, ©, The Oxford University Press, 1958, reprinted by permission.

There was always another scene that gives to these Low-Nile strands in the centre of Egypt their true and essential atmosphere. It was the black and white Pied kingfisher at work, one of the country's resident birds, much larger and plainer than the European kingfisher that one rarely sees so far south as Qena. As often as I recall my visits to this place the bird is hovering in its centre. A mile away the landing stage is visible but distorted in the mirage, and just this side of it a fisherman is slowly getting clearer as he walks towards me, casting out his circular net into the shallow water every fifty or hundred yards. In the foreground, quite near and untroubled by my presence, the kingfisher is hovering about ten feet above the water's edge, held stationary in the air by its vigorously flapping wings. Its head and beak are pointing straight down, as it watches the movement of each fish beneath the surface. Suddenly it drops head-first like a stone, submerging briefly with a splash to catch a fish in its bill or to rise without one and to start hovering again. . . . As it hovers again, you can walk up almost under it, but its wings are inaudible because of the wavelets at your feet. It seems to be about to dive; it is already beginning to fall, but at the last moment you can see the hesitation in its shoulders as it decides otherwise. The fish it was watching has moved away or perhaps it wasn't a fish at all, and the bird swings down sideways from its correct fishing height to rise in a curve and hover again a little farther along the strand.

Tunisia in the Spring

From *The Mediterranean,* by Alan Moorehead, in *Holiday,* copyright, 1954, by The Curtis Publishing Company, reprinted by permission of A. Watkins, Inc.

The perfect time to travel in Tunisia is in the spring. For some reason wildflowers blossom on that dry soil with an incredible African luxuriance. I remember one April driving forty miles from Kairouan in the center to Sousse on the coast, and never once did we see a patch of bare ground: the flowers rolled away in dizzy unbroken patterns to the horizon. Just at this time of the year there is a splendid trip to be made from Tunis. You cross the Cape Bon peninsula to Hammamet, a village of white beaches and transparent sea, and then turn south through Sousse for about 40 miles, until you reach El-Djem. This is one of the most surprising sights of the Mediterranean. In the middle of the empty featureless plain rises a mighty Roman amphitheatre. It is almost as big as the Colosseum and more perfectly preserved. You see it from miles off, and as you approach it seems to get bigger and bigger because there is nothing in the surrounding space with which to compare it. Perhaps because of this emptiness, there is a feeling of antiquity here stronger even than at Carthage. It is just one quick snapshot on the retina of the eye: just this one deserted monument in a void. If you climb to the topmost arches the view is still the same—nothing. And when you drive away you turn to look back with the uneasy feeling that something is unexplained—some unnatural gap in history has occurred and two thousand years have gone by without a word.

Sousse, Tunisia's Busy Port

From *Crossroads of the Mediterranean,* copyright, 1954, by Hendrik de Leeuw, reprinted by permission of Doubleday & Company, Inc., (Hanover House).

Sousse, an important and steadily growing port, with about as mixed a populace as one may see in any Mediterranean city, continued for many years, in days gone by, as a pirate's lair. The souks of Sousse are extremely fascinating, as is the port, which is made increasingly colorful by the diversified sails of Italian and Maltese fishing craft and dhows of Arabs, and the miscellaneous hotchpotch that associates itself always with any seaport. No less noteworthy is the great signal tower of the Citadel, a reconstructed pharos, or lighthouse, called Khalefel-Feta, which operated here in A.D. 1088. Finally there is the Kasbah, perched high on the hillside, overlooking from its loftiness the Arab quarter and souks. While Sousse cannot compete with Carthage in historical Roman interest, its claim to antiquity still admits few rivals. Founded in the ninth century B.C. as Hadrumetum, it is somewhat older than Carthage. . . . Hannibal retreated here after his defeat by Scipio in 203 B.C. . . . It succumbed at the order of Justinian to the army of Belisarius, was invaded by Arabs in A.D. 663, and after the defeat of the Byzantine army at Thysdrus (now known as El-Djem) in A.D. 689, it came under the hegemony of the caliphate at Bagdad. Such is the historical record of a place which under subsequent French direction has risen to become one of the most prosperous and busiest ports of Tunisia.

The Suks of Tunis

From *Introducing Africa,* copyright, 1954, by Carveth Wells, reprinted by permission of G. P. Putnam's Sons.

Tunisia's principal city is Tunis, situated at the end of a shallow lagoon so close to the sea as almost to be a part of the Mediterranean. A deep channel has been dredged across the lagoon to connect Tunis with the coastal town of La Goulette.

The most interesting feature of Tunis is the suks, little shops onto very narrow winding streets that are often roofed over. Many different kinds of craftsmen carry on their work here just as their forebears have done for centuries. The population of Tunis is 365,000 among whom are found about half the Italians, French, Jews, and Maltese of the protectorate.

Tunis can claim to have the most interesting and historic suburb in the world: the ancient city of Carthage, founded about 814 B.C. by the Phoenicians, destroyed for the first time by the Romans in 146 B.C., rebuilt by them, and finally destroyed by the Arabs in 698 A.D. On the site of the citadel stands today the Convent of the White Fathers, the residence and the cathedral of the Archbishop of Carthage, who is the Primate of all Africa.

The Ghosts of Carthage

From *Tunis,* by John Horne Burns, reprinted by special permission from *Holiday,* copyright, 1949, by The Curtis Publishing Company.

After the number of souvenirs you brought home as a veteran, and mindful of the torment of Latin II in high school, you swear you *won't* revisit Carthage. But you always end by boarding the mad electric train that runs down the main street of Tunis. After all, this is Sunday afternoon, and the round trip costs but 50 francs. You rattle across the strip of land bridging the Gulf of Tunis, and in twenty-seven minutes you're at Carthage. Just by scratching the red earth which buried the city you can bring up tiny green coins for your nephew in Hoboken: by soaking them three days in vinegar he will have a portrait of a Roman emperor, looking for all the world like Mussolini crowned with laurel. In Carthage you may be depressed by the sense of time and history that broods like a miasma over the Mediterranean area. On this now desolate plain 700,000 souls lived before the time of Christ. All that remains of them are columns, a broken amphitheater and some aqueducts. . . . *Delenda est Carthago!* So much vitality once in this desert by the blue sea, and now it's bones and amphorae under glass in a museum run by the White Fathers, with boxes for your voluntary contribution to further the work of excavation. A happier key is set by the evidences of Christianity, still very much alive on this spot. There's the Basilica of good Saint Louis. . . . and the Carmelite convent, from which no living nun emerges. And in the orchestra of the ruined amphitheater little girl orphans are playing basketball under the supervision of two nuns. But it's sunset. It's time to go back to still-living Tunis and drink lemonade on Avenue Jules Ferry.

Modern Algiers

From *Crossroads of the Mediterranean,* copyright, 1954, by Hendrik de Leeuw, reprinted by permission of Doubleday & Company, Inc., (Hanover House).

Algiers of today, a great and populous city, is a modern French town. The descendants of those corsairs to whom Europe once paid tribute mingle freely with the black-coated Frank, as though it were a privilege to breathe their native air. Algiers proper is the Icosium of the Romans, doubled, tripled, and quadrupled. Three towns in juxtaposition stretch from St. Eugène on the west to Mustapha on the east, while its heart lies in the Place du Gouvernement and the Grand Mosque. The Place du Gouvernement is a vast modern square, a sort of modern forum, flanked on one side by the Mosque of Djemael-Djedid—the Grand Mosque—on the other by shops, cafes, and hotels. Upon this square converge Bab-el-Oued, La Marine, La Kasbah, and Bab-Azoun, the four great thoroughfares of the city. All the animation and hubbub of the city center here, while the passing throng of Arabs, Mauresques, tribesmen, soldiers, and French and foreign nationals constitutes an ethnological entity as varied as it is unusual. Here all kinds of people of the East and West jostle one another good-naturedly, and the familiar vies with the unfamiliar in scenes bewildering to the eye. . . .

The city itself is replete with European innovations. Tramlines, highways, railroads, air lines are excellent and far-reaching. Transportation to Algeria on French, English, and American airplanes is extremely fast and comfortable. Air lines now reach into almost every corner of North Africa by TWA, Pan American, and Air France.

Street-Corner Pedagogy in Algiers

From *Algiers,* by John Horne Burns, reprinted by special permission from *Holiday,* copyright, 1949, by The Curtis Publishing Company.

The Main Drag of the splendid city of Algiers, recumbent on two hills, is like a serpent lashing his tail from the spacious port to the minareted mosques high in the trees at the top of the trough. On its lower levels it's called Rue Michelet, and it undulates by easy stages, always at a 30° angle, thrashing up the hill. After the fifth turn it becomes Boulevard Franklin D. Roosevelt. And three banks farther up it changes into the old Avenue of the Mission Saharienne, for from here—the site marked by a tiny white church—a little bevy of White Fathers went into the desert in 1889 to wrestle for souls.

Even the street signs are instructive: blue-and-white markers tell you something of each great man for whom the thoroughfares are named. In your walks you may learn, for example, the dates of the lifespan of Claude Debussy and that he was a French composer. The French have always been great ones for pedagogy in the open air; the best museums are out of doors. These wide plunging streets are sprayed each midnight by a sprinkler. They are planted from top to bottom of the town with dwarf evergreen trees, which by the street lights look like a stage set for a botanical garden.

Mozabite Cities

From *Places,* edited by Geoffrey Grigson and Charles Harvard Gibbs-Smith, reprinted by permission of Hawthorn Books, Inc., all rights reserved.

The M'zab, in Algeria, is a confederation of peculiar cities on the northern fringes of Sahara. There are five of them in all, built in a desolate region of bare limestone, cut by dry valleys, which give the arid landscape a net-like texture; and the Mozabites who inhabit them are members of the heretical Ibadi sect of Islam. Their strict acceptance of the Koran and rigid observance of dogma force them to be puritan and austere. Early in the tenth century they were persecuted and harassed by the orthodox. Forced to retreat farther and farther into the desert, at last they reached this desolate area, safe behind the rock and sand.

With the satellite cities of Bou-Noura, Melike, El Ateuf and Beni-Isguen all around within a few miles, the parent city of the group is Ghardaia. It stands on a hill, in a wide, sandy valley studded with rich palm groves, which creak characteristically with the noise of pulleys as mule and donkey draw up water from the deep wells. The houses are like boxes, pale blue, white and ochre, tier upon tier of them, piled up, and surmounted by a mosque with a pyramidal minaret; this form of minaret is peculiar to the Mozabites.

Constantine, the "City of the Air"

From *From Tangier to Tripoli,* copyright, 1923, by Frank G. Carpenter, reprinted by permission of Frances Carpenter Huntington and Doubleday & Company, Inc.

Constantine, Africa's famous city of the air . . . lies in the heart of North Africa about three hundred miles east of Algiers, fifty miles south of the Mediterranean, and one hundred and twenty-five miles north of the Desert of Sahara. It is built upon an enormous rock at an altitude of two thousand feet above the sea, and nearly encircling it is a mighty gorge a thousand feet deep. The houses stand on a huge stone platform on three sides of which rocky walls drop down precipitously to a valley almost twice as deep as the Washington Monument is high. A rushing, foaming river flows through the gorge thus made. On every side lies a rolling country ending in the desert-like mountains of the great Atlas chain. I doubt whether there is another such city on earth. The Arabs call it "The City of the Air," and it is the mightiest roof garden known to man. The Kasbah or citadel . . . commands the highest point on the rocky plateau and is above the most precipitous part of the gorge. In it there are stone cisterns and granaries built by the Romans, while not far from it is a great stone aqueduct which the Romans made to supply the place with water. . . . The gorge is about two hundred feet wide, narrowing in places to one hundred and fifty feet or less. The rocks rise almost straight up from the river. . . . Down in the gorge the noises of the city are unheard, and nothing breaks the stillness but the whirring of the wings of the crows, storks, and other birds, as they fly across to their nests in one wall or the other, and the roaring of the hurrying river as it dashes on through the rocks.

ASIA

On the following double-page spread is a photograph of the Basilica of the Agony in the Garden of Gethsemane on the Mount of Olives. This is a treasured place for Christians.

The Garden of Gethsemane

From *Strange Lands and Friendly People,* copyright, 1951, by William O. Douglas, reprinted by permission of Harper & Brothers.

At the bottom of the Mount of Olives is Gethsemane, the garden where He was wont to pray and where He was betrayed by Judas. Now as then it is an olive grove; and today the olive trees are relics of an ancient age. Their trunks are gnarled, twisted, and hollowed, and many times thicker than any I had seen. A Franciscan church is located in the garden; and one of its Fathers (whose name I never knew) spoke feelingly of the olives. This man, like the olive trees, was aged. I asked him how old he thought the trees were. Though he had doubtless been asked the same question a thousand times, he stood in reflection awhile and then reverently replied, "I have come to believe they were young trees when Christ first came here to pray."

We crossed the Valley of Judgment below us on the west. It seemed that each available plot of ground was already occupied by a grave. Tombstones are packed tight through the whole reach of the valley and on both slopes. It is an odd-looking cemetery. There is no expanse of trees, no green lawns to break the desolation of the spot.

The First Time I Saw Jerusalem

From *A Pilgrim's Vow,* ©, 1956, by Pierre van Paassen, reprinted by permission of The Dial Press.

It was the hour when the evening star comes out. A cool breeze, harbinger of night, had begun to blow from the east, carrying a faint scent of jasmine and violet from the desert. We could see the hills around and about Jerusalem, rose-colored, with mauve pockets where the shadows were falling. Straight ahead of us appeared the massive silhouette of the Dome of the Rock. All of us in the station wagon grew silent as imagination or memory spun out the threads of sacred history leading to and from the monument. For, on that site, on Mount Moriah, which was hallowed ground even before Jerusalem received its name, Abraham's hand was stayed as he was about to sacrifice his son Isaac. There also, Solomon built the first Temple of Yahveh; and Herod, the second more splendid one. Above the great Mosque, which has taken the place of the Temple, we could see a slight haze, the merest wisp of silver gossamer, trembling against the gloaming east. Thus Jesus must have seen the pillar of smoke rise from God's altars as the last strains of the evening prayer trailed off into the unfathomable silence of the night.

The biblical expression of going to the Holy City is to "go up" to Jerusalem. The faithful from all over Palestine and adjacent territories "went up" on the occasion of the great religious and national festivals of Passover and Tabernacles. It is written that David "went up," that Jesus and his disciples "went up." The same verb is used to describe a priest's ascent of the steps of the altar. The relevancy of this expression became evident as we drew nearer and nearer to the Holy City and one gained the impression of entering a purer realm, a spirtually-pervaded atmosphere.

The Souks of Baghdad

From *From An Antique Land,* copyright, 1954, by Julian Huxley, reprinted by permission of Crown Publishers, Inc., and Max Parrish & Co., Ltd.

The Souks or covered Bazaars of Baghdad are famous, and rightly so. They seem more extensive and spacious than those of Damascus or Istanbul. The adjacent Street of the Coppersmiths is perhaps even more impressive. There, after walking down a few steps from street level, you can see craftsmen actually at work, and arrays of their gleaming products, like the big brass trays on which the visitor to Arab tents finds a mound of rice and moutton awaiting his fingers. And the clangor and the cool but dusty dimness give the place an unforgettable quality. My wife once witnessed five sturdy men, bared to the waist, beating out a copper plate with long-handled hammers. The five hammers came down time after time on the same spot in rapid rhythmic sequence. She could hardly tear herself away from the spectacle, which has remained one of her most vivid memories.

I liked the tailors in the Bazaar, sitting cross-legged in the proper fashion for tailors, on raised platforms beside the thronged alleys, stitching and talking busily, equally prepared to make a European or an Oriental suit of clothes.

On the following double-page spread is a photograph of the Temple of Jain in Calcutta. This is one of the most beautiful of the 20 Jain temples in the city.

A Jain Temple In Calcutta

From *Altars of the East,* copyright ©, 1956, by Lew Ayres, reprinted by permission of Doubleday & Company, Inc.

Back in Calcutta we wound up affairs and prepared to move on to Benares. The last night brought us a complete worship service in one of the Jain temples. They opened all doors and showed us many phases of their particular liturgy. So clean and elegant was the marble interior, with jeweled images and other priceless treasures enshrined, that an armed guard stands perpetually in the doorway with bayonet-tipped rifle at port arms. Needless to mention, he is not a Jain. The Jains themselves are non-violent. Before approaching the altar for worship the Jain lay follower will enter a small chamber off the entrance for the purpose of bathing the entire body and making a complete change of clothing. Shoes are never worn inside.

One unusual type of individual worship consists of kneeling by a small table before the image and laying out an intricate design with grains of rice. When the figure is finished, it will be decorated with different fruits and nuts, forming a very interesting, often beautiful pattern, somewhat in the manner of a Navaho sand painting, though not as primitive or as colorful. Each element of the design symbolizes another promise of virtue. Each placement of a fruit is a dedication of effort and devotion. Some were bizarre, many fanciful; it was fascinating to watch these strange creations take place under the deft hands of an artistic worshiper.

Calcutta—"The City of Palaces"

From *The Land and People of India,* by H. G. Rawlinson, E.I.E., reprinted by permission of The Macmillan Company and A. and C. Black Ltd.

This great city, with its host of buildings extending for many miles along the banks of the river Ganges, was once, some 250 years ago, a group of fever-stricken, swampy islands, the haunt of tigers and other wild animals, about 100 miles from the mouth of the Hooghly.

Its importance as a trading station for merchandise from the rich province of Bengal was first recognized by a British merchant named Job Charnock, who, in spite of refusals, at length obtained from the Nawab or Viceroy of Bengal permission in 1690 to build a factory, which he named Fort William, after King William III. The fort, with its battlemented walls, still stands on the west of the Maidan Park, facing the waterside. Behind it is Chowringhee, with many handsome buildings which have earned for Calcutta the title of "the city of palaces." The view, especially at sunset, of the mass of shipping from all parts of the world lying in the stream as far as Garden Reach, and of the Botanical Gardens, Fort William, and the Esplanade, is very striking. Straight ahead stands the Victoria Memorial, dedicated by Lord Curzon to the first Empress of India. The white marble dome, gleaming in the sun, is crowned by a figure of Victory 16 feet high. The galleries contain a unique collection of historical pictures, an oriental library, and many busts of members of the British Royal Family and of Viceroys and other distinguished men.

The Taj Mahal

From *A Writer's Notebook,* copyright, 1949, by W. Somerset Maugham, reprinted by permission of Doubleday & Company, Inc., the author and Messrs. Heinemann.

Notwithstanding my expectation and all the pictures I had seen of it, when I got my first and proper view of it, the view from the terrace of the gateway, I was overcome by its beauty. I recognized that this was the authentic thrill of art and tried to examine it in myself while it was still vivid. I can understand that when people say something takes their breath away it is not an idle metaphor. I really did feel shortness of breath. I had a queer, delightful feeling in my heart; as though it were dilated. I felt surprise and joy and, I think, a sense of liberation; but I had just been reading the Samkhya philosophy in which art is regarded as a temporary liberation of the same sort as that absolute liberation in which all Indian religion ends, so it may be that this was no more than a reminiscence that I transferred to my actual feeling.

I cannot enjoy the same ecstasy over a beautiful thing twice over, and next day when I went to the Taj again, at the same hour, it was only with my mind that I enjoyed the same sight. On the other hand I got something else. As the sun was setting I wandered into the Mosque. I was quite alone. As I looked from one end along the chambers into which it is divided I had an eerie, mysterious sense of its emptiness and silence. I was a trifle scared. I can only put what I felt into words that make no sense: I seemed to hear the noiseless footfall of the infinite.

Old Delhi

From *This Is India,* by Santha Rama Rau. Copyright, 1953, by The Curtis Publishing Company, reprinted by permission of Harper & Brothers.

Although the seat of the government is in New Delhi in the brash new buildings, it is Old Delhi, only a few miles away, that has not only the fascinating bazaars, but also such nationally famous places as the Jama Masjid—a huge and beautiful mosque—and the Red Fort and the Kashmir Gate. There, too, inside the walls of the old city, you will see the humming life of the Indian sidewalks. Early in the morning there may be the village women who have been walking since four or five o'clock to bring their fruit, flowers and vegetables into town, and they will transform the street into a market. Later in the morning those stalls will have vanished and perhaps basketmakers, or men making children's toys out of colored paper or a few palm leaves, will have taken over. In the early afternoon the street will be deserted except for a few coolies sleeping in the shade of the wall. By evening there may be sweet stalls, people selling betel nuts, a man with a traveling tea urn and little metal cups which he clinks together to attract your attention, or a stall with the heavy, pervasive *attars* of musk or rose or jasmine for which Delhi is famous.

Festival in India

From *Strange Lands and Friendly People,* copyright, 1951, by William O. Douglas, reprinted by permission of Harper & Brothers.

I was in Almora during the festival of Nanda Devi. This town is located on a ridge facing snowy sentinels of the Himalayas that mount higher in the sky than any peak on the North American continent. The day I was in Almora there was dancing in the streets. Men and boys with flutes and bagpipes gathered crowds in the courtyard of the temple and on street corners, where they played wild, exotic tunes. Everyone was happy. Thousands filled the town; they were packed in the streets and the bazaars; they sat on roofs in bright-colored clothes waiting for the procession. It was a joyful, milling crowd out on a holiday, such as we find in our county fairs. . . . There was an excellent display of local products. Government experimental stations had exhibits, showing fruits and vegetables. . . . Vocational schools showed woodwork, needlework, weaving; villagers brought in beautiful hand-woven shawls and cloth. A young Indian veterinarian had a stall showing the scientific way to prevent and treat the dread liver fluke among cattle. . . . It was an enthusiastic community outpouring. . . . It was somehow the spirit of a new India— the tireless energy of millions dedicated to a challenging and vast undertaking. Ancient hand skills, new technology, and modern science were combined to make public an interesting progress report. And yet it was all done under the auspices of Nanda Devi, a goddess born of myth and integrated into the Hindu religious system of thought.

Land of the Abominable Snowman

From *India,* by Robert C. Kingsbury, copyright ©, 1957, by Nelson Doubleday, Inc., reprinted by permission.

The Himalaya, the "abode of snow," is the most fomidable of all mountain ranges. More than twenty snow-capped giants higher than Mt. McKinley, the highest mountain in North America, tower into the skies. Everest, the world's highest peak, has been conquered, but a host of others have never been climbed by man. This is the home of the abominable snowman, that legendary creature of the high snows whose large humanlike footprints, but no other trace, are often encountered by Himalayan expeditions. Mountain resort towns like Darjeeling, Naini Tal, and Simla were developed by the British to escape the fierce spring and summer heat of the plains. Indeed, the entire national government used to migrate to Simla when 110° in New Delhi proved too impossible. The present Indian government, however, remains in its capital and fittingly perspires with the rest of the nation. The hill stations, though losing much of their glitter with the British exodus, are still well patronized by wealthy Indians and Western diplomats, missionaries, and businessmen. Comfortable old hotels and magnificent mountain scenery are their special forte. From Ranikhet and Darjeeling, the sweeping panorama of the perpetual snows and glaciers of the Himalaya is especially superb.

Benares—Holy City

From *Edward Lear's Indian Journal,* by Edward Lear, edited by Ray Murphy, reprinted by permission of Jarrolds Publishers (London) Ltd.

Utterly wonderful is the rainbow-like edging of the water with thousands of bathers reflected in the river. Then the color of the temples, the strangeness of the huge umbrellas and the inexpressibly multitudinous detail of architecture, costume, etc. . . . How well I remember the views of Benares by Daniell, R. A.; pallid, gray, sad, solemn. I had always supposed this place a melancholy, or at least a staid and soberly-colored spot, a gray record of bygone days. Instead, I find it one of the most abundantly *bruyant,* and startlingly radiant of places full of bustle and movement. Constantinople or Naples are simply dull and quiet by comparison. . . . About 1:30 or 2, after having sate in the boat doubled up to avoid the hot sun, and gazing at the wondrous world of bathers, huddled close together, or shewing themselves singly to the devout multitude of Benares, I began a drawing of the temples which I had vainly tried yesterday, and managed to get what, should photographs be obtainable, may one day prove more or less useful. The mealy man of meditation came to the surface, and stood for a time wildly acting, and apparently intending a header, but he subsided into squatting and lute-playing; today he sports a feeble bit of string as dress. Many corpses are carried to burn at these steps. Some buffalo and human corpses are thrown into the water; big black vultures congregate thereon, with no end of black crows. The pretty myna birds are numerous everywhere; pigeons by the 10,000,000. At 3, finished my last Benares drawing and am truly glad to have seen this wonderful place. Then paid the boatman 2 rs., and came to the garry. Near the temple, apes abound, crawling all over walls, and along the road, and up the trees, no end of brutes.

Bombay Night Scene

From *The Menacing Sun,* by Mona Gardner, copyright, 1939, by Harcourt, Brace and Company, Inc., reprinted by permission.

There is no hush at nightfall in Bombay. The noises of the day go right on and become the noises of the night. They alter and shift, but they never grow less. Just at dusk the crows toss in the sky and scream a fury of resentment before they settle like a malignant shroud over the trees. But when they are quiet there is a gathering flood of human voices that swells and rolls down each street and alley, for those who have been in offices and stores and kitchens all day come out at night into the open to merge with the others who are always there. They walk and argue in thick throngs around old men stretched out on cots, past stools and chairs. . . .

There is laughter, but not much song. A flute may sound its eerie minors and, across the night, another one may answer in the same sensuous melancholy; and with it the pulse-beat of a drum. But no one sings with these: no one throws back his head in sheer exuberance with the necessity for song. Over on the lawn of the Yacht Club an orchestra plays temperate Viennese waltzes and these sift out along the sea-wall. . . .

Lahore

From *Horned Moon,* by Ian Stephens, reprinted by permission of Indiana University Press.

In March the nights at Lahore are cool, the afternoons agreeably warm; blossom scents the air. At dawn, the gentle notes of doves and hoopoes rouse one. . . . Along the canal bank, the tall silk-cotton trees, with buttressed grey boles, were in profusion of scarlet blossom. The flowers stuck out brilliantly from bare branches; the new leaves would come later.

Villagers wearing coloured shawls swung their legs at evening on the balustrade of a bridge. There was a murmur of gossip. A hookah was being smoked, its aromatic fumes over-sweet. . . . Green parakeets dashed screeching across the twilit sky, their long tails rigid. By the next bridge a singer of religious poems and two drummers sat in the dust. I went back in gathering darkness. The moon came up. White blossom on a small orange tree perfumed the air.

As I paused at the door, beautifully piercing the silence came the purity of a passing villager's flute; a few simple notes, repeated. The small, clear sound afloat in the night wrung the heart; all life's pathos somehow lay in it.

Customs of Karachi

From *McKay's Guide to the Far East and the Middle East,* copyright, 1953, 1956, by Eleanor Cowles Gellhorn, reprinted by permission of David Mc-Kay Company, Inc.

In the early eighteenth century, Karachi was no more than an insignificant fishing village. It has now developed into a large city of nearly a million and a half people, largely on account of the onslaught of political and religious immigrants and refugees. It is still a fast-growing city, but it has yet to catch up with itself. The city is flat and sprawling and drab but with nice wide streets and some handsome public buildings. It has gradually developed a fine and important harbor. There has been tremendous and ever increasing industrial expansion in Karachi, which has become a great air center with the biggest airport in Asia.

Being Moslem, the women for the most part observe purdah (seclusion, faces veiled), but this is changing rapidly. The custom of dying the palms of the hands and the finger tips a henna red still persists among the lower classes. The national costume for the women for formal dress is the *gharara;* for less formal dress the *camiz,* a long shirt, over the *shalwar,* a divided full-length skirt, or trousers. The head cloth, which is long enough to fall over the shoulders, is called a *dopatta. Burka* is the name of the heavy veil with which women cover themselves from head to feet. These have two tiny embroidered holes in the face area, to see through.

The national costume for men consists of a *sherwani,* a long frock with a closed upstanding collar, and *shalwar,* or pajama trousers, and a Jinnah cap. Western clothing is much used, also.

East and West Pakistan—A Study in Contrast

From *The Road to Shali-mar,* by Carveth Wells, copyright, 1952, by Zetta Wells, reprinted by permission.

The outstanding feature of East Pakistan is its network of mighty rivers, the Ganges, the Brahmaputra, and their many tributaries. In one area the Ganges is ten miles wide! These rivers not only bring down vast quantities of ferti-lizing silt which is deposited over the surface of the land, but they contain an inexhaustible supply of fish. . . .

In the south are the famous Sundarbans, dense tropical jungles which abound in big game, including the Bengal tiger, leopard, bear, wild boar, and many other animals.

East Pakistan is served by Chittagong, often called the "Port of Destiny." Until firm and friendly relations are established between Pakistan and India, trade communications between West and East Pakistan are by sea and air. Fortunately for Pakistan, the products of East Pakistan are different from those of West Pakistan, and each part wants what the other produces. Conse-quently ships that load up with cargoes in Karachi, destined for Chittagong, do not return empty, but loaded to the water line with goods produced in East Pakistan and needed by the people of West Pakistan. . . .

The climates of East and West Pakistan are as different as their principal products. West Pakistan, generally speaking, is cold in winter and hot during the summer, but this extreme climate is bracing and dry, making the inhabi-tants strong and sturdy.

East Pakistan is warm and humid, with an average rainfall that in many places is at least ten times as great as that in West Pakistan. But there is one feature that is common to both East and West Pakistan. The nights are gen-erally cool, making it easy to sleep.

Strikingly different in products and climate, East and West Pakistan are just as different in the appearance of their inhabitants. West Pakistan is a land of tall men with high cheekbones who often sport large black mustaches and wear turbans, baggy trousers, and speak Urdu, whereas in East Pakistan the men are short, bearded, wear skirts, skullcaps, and speak Bengali.

On the following double-page spread is a photograph of Bangkok, Thailand,
from the Temple of Dawn whose 245-foot tower gives a magnificent view of the city.

The Temples of Bangkok

From *McKay's Guide to The Far East and The Middle East,* copyright, 1953, by Eleanor Cowles Gellhorn, reprinted by permission of David Mc-Kay Company, Inc.

There is no more entrancing sight in all the world than the temples of Bangkok. Don't miss it. . . . Bangkok itself is a huge, flat city—like a lot of small villages thrown together, with residences and shops and offices in each section. The buildings are a mixture of the very old and the very new, as are the houses. Many of the houses are made of teakwood and roofed with thatch or red tile and shaped more or less in a simplified version of the Siamese temple. There are endless canals winding through the city; many of the houses that line them are built on posts or supported by floats. And again, as in Hong Kong, one finds families living permanently on their sampans, which clog the canals. The streets are bedlam—crammed with busses and automobiles, bicycles and *samlors*—the three-wheel bicycle rickshaws—which are delightfully clean and shining and multicolored.

Walking the streets of Bangkok, one gets the impression, at first, of drabness, but the startling brilliance and beauty and fascination of the almost endless temples scattered throughout its area make one come away from there with the conviction that Bangkok is the most colorful and enchanting city in the whole wide world.

The Floating Market of Bangkok

From *The Innocent Ambassadors,* copyright ©, 1957, by Philip Wylie, reprinted by permission of Rinehart & Company, Inc.

Ricky and I boated through the floating market of Bangkok in a low-powered, double-prowed craft with a brass engine that looked like Japanese handiwork. A wooden awning shaded us; we had a boy aboard to help with landings, a man to steer—and Charlie to tell all. I will not ever forget those people who lived on water streets. Everybody bathed and all the kids swam at their own doorsteps. Each merchant—seller of hot coffee or ice, yard goods, coal, wood or hardware—had a small boat painted an identifying color. Each also had a gong, bell, drum or rattle that announced his type of wares, as he approached. The supermarket in Bangkok comes to *you*.

Some canal-fronting homes bore street numbers; and there were electric "street lights" overhead. We even witnessed the house-to-house calls of a meter reader from the local power company: he was also water-borne. Greybeards and grandmas, infants, teen-agers, lovely girls smiled as we passed, laughed with us, and waved until our arms were weary from waving back, our faces stiff from smiling. To go out on the veranda, work a while at a collection of potted orchids and then descend, clothes and all, into the warm, muddy water —washing self and garments in the same bath . . . what a life! Boys and girls performed show-off tricks for us like kids everywhere—diving from a porch rail, swimming under water, catching hold of our boat and letting it tow them. And in that verdant Venice no one appeared destitute, yet none was rich. There seemed to be no sad people.

The Shwe Dagon Pagoda

From *Full Moon in Burma,* by Nancy Wilson Ross, copyright, 1954, by The New Yorker Magazine, Inc., reprinted by permission of the publisher.

The Shwe Dagon Pagoda stands on a very ancient sacred site. The Pagoda dates back to 588 B. C. There has been no major change in its size or shape since 1564. Once the British tried to carry the Pagoda's great bell off to Calcutta. While they were attempting to put it aboard ship, it fell into the river, and the British could not raise it. Then—the story goes—certain pious Burmese went to the British and said, "Since you can't get the great bell from the temple onto your ship, will you let us have it back if we can rescue it from the river?" The British gave their consent. By superhuman efforts, and using only the most primitive means, the Burmese managed to raise the great bell from the river bed and hang it again in the Pagoda.

The Pagoda is not only the center of Rangoon life but a central point of worship for all Burma, and beyond. It has also served many times as a refuge from attacking forces, including the Japanese in the last war, when the local populace huddled among the smiling images of their Prince of Peace as the bombs fell. The Pagoda is vast, impressive, confused, yet curiously serene. All around a central terrace there is a riot of heterogeneous images and many different shrines, varying in concept from good taste to marked vulgarity. Some have fallen into shocking disrepair; others are bright with newly applied gold leaf, which is sold in small strips in the market stalls and applied by the pious to any spot they choose. I began to feel, as I wandered with Diana, that it might be this very range of optic impression that gives the Pagoda its strangely moving total effect, subtly reminding the devout of the uncertain tides of men and, by contrast, the eternally surviving principles of the Law, the Doctrine, and the Brotherhood.

On the following double-page spread is a photograph of the teeming, colorful port of Hong Kong, considered by many to be one of the most beautiful in the world.

View from the Peak

From *Hong Kong,* by Han Suyin, in *Holiday,* copyright, 1955, by The Curtis Publishing Company, reprinted by permission of the author.

Where can one get a good view of Hong Kong? Why, from the Peak. The Peak is a physical landmark, and a spiritual symbol. Although merely eighteen hundred feet high, it is ten degrees cooler than the city below, and its slopes are so steep above the city that it looks higher. A small climbing tramway takes you to the top in ten minutes; gradually the city recedes, shrinks, and its peaceful hubbub dies away. The public garden, with its prehistoric fern trees like gigantic, inefficient umbrellas, its fountain and the happy Chinese children around it; Government House, which looks like a Californian bungalow with palm trees and a tower—all shrink to doll size. On either side of our climbing train the houses appear and then recede. They and their gardens lean perilously, it seems, from the hillside. The flowerpots and the frangipani and honeysuckle clusters in the gardens wave delicious fragrance in our faces as we go past. The steep gullies carved by rain in the hillside are filled with dense jungle and add a touch of wildness to an otherwise trim, civilized landscape. Up and up we climb, stopping only where a curve of the winding road comes close to the tracks. Here passengers disembark at higher and yet higher levels.

The Colony unfolds itself, a breath-taking sight, like nothing in the world except perhaps the Bay of Rio de Janeiro. Across the harbor rise the Dragon Hills and other ranges, blue and gray and glinting with gold, sparkling with pink and magenta shadows at dawn and evening. All around is sea, peacock blue and gold sea, and the seventy-five islands rising from it, like calm ships, forever changing their colors as the sun strikes them or leaves them in shade, or as clouds float by.

Hong Kong

From *Any Old Place With You,* copyright ©, 1957, by William K. Zinsser, reprinted by permission of Simon and Schuster, Inc.

The colony of Hong Kong consists of one peninsula, Kowloon, which juts off the mainland of Communist China, and dozens of smaller islands. The most famous of these is the "Rock" popularized by Han Suyin's *A Many-Splendored Thing* and various movies. Along its waterfront are clustered the great offices of British trade, like Jardine, Matheson & Co., Butterfield and Swire, and Thos. Cook & Son. The streets run sharply upward, and on the hill behind are the genteel houses of the rich, overlooking the loveliest harbor in the world.

To reach the city you must cross by ferry from Kowloon, where the plane lands. It is an enchanted boat ride. The ferry leaves every ten minutes and it has the same restless beat as Hong Kong itself. Rich and poor crowd on, carrying bundles and babies, impatient as New Yorkers in rush hour.

There were hundreds of boats—battleships, ocean liners and freighters, junks with reddish sails, tubs pieced together from rusty scrap iron, sampans big enough for one family or one man.

Manila, Tumultuous Mixture

From *View to the Southeast,* by Santha Rama Rau, copyright, 1955, by The Curtis Publishing Company, reprinted by permission of Harper & Brothers.

Of all the many influences that have reached the Philippines, the most recent and in many ways the most effective has been the American. Like the Spanish rulers, the Americans made Manila their headquarters and it is in the capital that one sees the most obvious signs of American influence; from Manila American ways of thinking and living, American gadgets or policies spread unevenly to the rest of the country. This newest layer of history has added another dimension to a city that already is a composite of a dozen civilizations.

This tumultuous mixture of races and cultures and personalities is perhaps the first aspect of Manila that impresses the visitor. The wide green boulevard that follows the beautiful curve of Manila Bay (one of the world's largest and best harbors) is named for Admiral Dewey. As you move away from the clean American lines of the sea front, you will find streets and squares with Spanish names crisscrossed with, say, Nebraska or Tennessee Street, or with the brave names of the Philippines' own heroes, Rizal, Quezon, Mabini. In Manila you can lead an entirely Spanish life, if you desire, among the large community of Spanish businessmen, officials, visitors and journalists. . . . Equally, you can lead an American life with all the necessary surroundings of American clubs, restaurants, soda fountains, movies, plays and people. Or a Chinese life. Or even, in a small way, an Indian life.

On the following double-page spread is a photograph of the feudal castle at Hirosaki, north of Tokyo, its beauty enhanced by April cherry blossoms.

Train from Tokyo

From *The Cingalese Prince,* copyright, 1934, by Brooks Atkinson, reprinted by permission of Doubleday & Company, Inc.

Everyone in Tokyo appeared to be going somewhere. . . . For half an hour before the train left, the platform was crowded with a multitude of well-wishers, some in native dress, some in formal Western attire, but all bowing deeply and modestly with a grace that made Europeans look boorish. . . . When the train pulled out, the gentlemen raised their hats and bowed courteously, and the kimonoed ladies bowed deeply from the waist; and although we were not included in the civilities we felt that we were leaving good friends behind. . . .

The heavy, luxuriously equipped train raced through towns and villages and through miles and miles of rice fields where coolies, wearing enormous straw hats, were cultivating their crops. Houses and barns, thatched huts, orchards, shrines, and farmyards ran like a kaleidoscope past the windows. The train began to climb into the mountains. I gazed rhapsodically at the thickly matted white clouds that swam across the mountains and rose to amazing heights. Never had clouds revealed such daring architecture before. Never had they raised a crest with so much grandeur into the sky, beseeching the gods for mercy. Suddenly I saw that I was wrong; I could have cried with excitement. It was not a cloud dome. It was Fujiyama. The white, unwrinkled cone with its torn summit was the sacred mountain of this pulsating island. Above the clouds it rose with a gigantic reach of supplication into the sun of a May morning, where the necessities of a nation were beyond sight and sound.

Traditional New Year's Day Breakfast

From *Chiyo's Return,* by Chiyono Sugimoto Kiyooka, copyright, 1935, by Doubleday & Company, Inc., reprinted by permission of the publisher.

The soup (called *ozoni*—which means "mixed,") contained many vegetables each of which was a good-luck symbol for the future. All the plates and bowls were of lacquer, as nothing breakable is ever used on New Year's Day. . . . In the separate boxes were tiny dried fish wrapped in seaweed, red-brown roe, large sweet black beans, and mochi prepared in a dozen different forms.

There must always be plenty of mochi in every house for New Year's. Those big flat cakes of rice paste which we had seen pounded and rolled out had been cut into dozens of pieces to be used for little blocks in soup, dumplings to cook with vegetables, small balls rolled in sweet pea-powder or prepared with an outside of bean and spices, delicious to the tongue of every nation.

A little later, a small tray was brought in on which was a low, odd-shaped sort of teapot with a long slender spout. On the cover was fastened an elaborate decoration of white and red paper, folding in bits of pine, bamboo, and plum blossoms. It held *toso*—an old-fashioned herb-flavored rice wine which, in serving, was carefully poured in three short tip-ups of a few drops into a shallow cup.

The Heart of Tokyo

From *Japan,* edited by Doré Ogrizek, copyright in Great Britain, 1957, reprinted by permission of McGraw-Hill Book Company, Inc.

Anyone who arrives in Haneda, the airport of Tokyo, and continues by car to the center of the capital, would tend to believe through his half-hour drive that the town had been laid out according to a definite plan. In summertime the most propitious moment for this excursion is shortly after sunrise. At this hour the heat is still dry, and in the wide, straight, dusty avenues there are as yet few, if any, cyclists—a permanent menace in Japan. To the right and left are buildings of wood or brick, occasionally crested with a terrace, and ornamented with inscriptions of Chinese characters which are surprisingly decorative although they merely advertise laundries, grocers' stores, carpenters' workshops, electricians' or radio repairers' booths. Above many of the doorways hang lanterns of paper and bamboo, red, green, or orange in color, shaped like gourds, melons, or pumpkins as the case may be. But despite the apparently strict observance of alignment, this facade is merely a decoy behind which thousands of houses (if such is the word) huddle together in a chaos which defies all description. Then, almost without transition, "real" buildings of stone suddenly loom up, six, seven, or eight storeys high, in blocks intersected by temples, sportsgrounds and parks (of which there are 215 in Tokyo, big and small alike). Unhappily what the architecture loses in quaintness is by no means gained in beauty. At a crossroads carefully guarded by a policeman—the absolute dictator of traffic—the sun gently dances on the roofs of the Imperial Palace. There beats the heart of this city, capital of the Empire since 1868 only.

Kyoto, the Boston of Japan

From *Japan,* by James A. Michener, reprinted by special permission from *Holiday,* copyright, 1952, by The Curtis Publishing Company.

Kyoto . . . is a large, spacious city laid out as a replica of a Chinese metropolis. For over a thousand years Kyoto served as the capital of Japan. It is the center of Buddhism, the repository of national culture. Say the Japanese, "You might call it our Boston." Kyoto has more than 800 temples and shrines, and dozens of small shops where ancient handicrafts are carried on as they were 400 years ago. One excellent establishment makes wood-block prints and you can see how as many as forty different blocks of wood are kept in perfect register.

Four things should be seen in Kyoto: the ancient palace of the emperors, the old castle of the feudal lords where floor boards have built-in squeaks called "antiassassination whispers," the broad gardens of the Heian shrine, where Japan's finest cherry blossoms bloom, and—most remarkable of them all—the temple containing 1001 life-size, eleven-faced, thousand-handed gilt statues of the Chinese goddess Kwannon.

129

Japanese Gardens in Kyoto

From *Kyoto,* by Robert Sherrod in *The Saturday Evening Post,* copyright, 1954, by The Curtis Publishing Company, reprinted by permission.

The Japanese garden is a carefully planned landscape, frequently in delightful diminutive, containing stunted trees, a miniature lake featuring a miniature bridge or a miniature boat. In all cases proportion is the alpha and the omega. Rocks are more important than flowers, particularly rocks that are shaped like a living creature; in the Emperor's private garden there is a noble, low-lying turtle. The test of artistry among the Japanese lies in the arrangement of the rocks.

Running water, the symbol of purity, is better than still water. Moss—*koke* in Japanese—is preferred to grass, and many authorities consider the Moss Temple Garden, covered with an undulating carpet of emerald, bronze and jade moss, the most exquisite in all Japan; the Buddhist priest who designed it, Muso Kokushi, is regarded after six centuries as one of Japan's foremost artists.

Other fanciers nominate the Silver Pavilion, another small garden featuring two huge piles of white sand and an irregular pond set against the green hillside of Higashiyama, thereby leading the eye naturally to the skyline; whereas Western gardens are usually designed to be viewed from above, Japanese gardens often require an upward viewing, which is not difficult in mountain-hemmed Kyoto.

Illumination of Nara's Kasuga Shrine

From *Japan and America,* by Henry W. Taft, copyright, 1932, by The Macmillan Company, reprinted by permission.

Perhaps the most moving experience of our visit to Japan was the illumination of the ancient stone lanterns around the Kasuga Shrine. A long ascending avenue with occasional flights of stone steps is enclosed by parallel rows of stone lanterns crowded together so thickly that scarcely any intervening space is left. They are all of pagoda shape with a single set of curved eaves or projections and windows with heavy stone grilling for the effect when lighted within. Most of the lanterns are said to be over a thousand years old. In the cloister-like enclosures of the neighboring temples there are also bronze lanterns suspended by chains and of great variety of designs, but all having their sides of decorated grill work. All of the lanterns are either votive offerings or memorials erected at private expense. There are 2000 stone lanterns and 1500 of bronze. A wick floating in oil furnishes light. All the lanterns are regularly lighted twice a year, but our visit was made the occasion of a special illumination. A misty rain was falling. Through the grilled sides of the lanterns in spreading rays the light struggled through the surrounding gloom, having a special effect not conducive to levity. Indeed, our slow march through the vast eerie precinct where thousands of feeble tapers vainly "burn dim, like lamps in noisome air," was one of the most impressive episodes of our visit, and quite unique.

The Geishas

From *East of Home,* copyright, 1950, by Santha Rama Rau, reprinted by permission of Harper & Brothers.

Our Kyoto visit ended with a dinner given for us by Mr. Kaku, a business friend of my father, in one of the famous old restaurants of the city. . . . Since the geishas are mainly entertainers they can choose their lovers to the degree that they are valuable as artists. A very great singer, for instance, cannot be bought because her income from her music, from records, and public or private performances is great enough to give her complete independence. All the great women artists were trained from among the geishas until now. . . .

Besides the geishas there were four of five maikos brought in to entertain us. The maiko, literally "a dancing child," is twelve to fifteen in age. . . . They are a sort of apprentice geisha and get their education and training in art in the geisha house and under the protection of the older geishas. It is a system which seems to the Western mind rather shocking, yet compared with what some children can expect should they stay with their very poor families or in the villages, it has its compensations.

In contrast with the simple sober-colored kimonos of the older geisha, the maiko wears brilliant silks with wide elaborate obis in gold and brocade. . . . The geishas unobstrusively but most efficiently helped one to eat, saw that more was brought of any dish you particularly liked, took the bones out of the fish for you, kept your cup full of warmed wine, and made conversation on whatever subject you showed an interest in. Between courses they sang for us and danced the formal, slow-moving Japanese dances. The maikos did rather gayer dances than the geishas and seemed to enjoy themselves enormously.

The Japanese Landscape

From *Glimpses of Unfamiliar Japan,* copyright, 1894, by Lafcadio Hearn.

There is a strange, wild, dark beauty in Japanese landscapes, a beauty not easily defined in words. The secret of it must be sought in the extraordinary lines of the mountains, in the strangely abrupt crumpling and jagging of the ranges; no two masses closely resembling each other, every one having a fantasticality of its own. Where the chains reach to any considerable height, softly swelling lines are rare: the general characteristic is abruptness, and the charm is the charm of Irregularity.

Doubtless this weird Nature first inspired the Japanese with their unique sense of the value of irregularity in decoration,—taught them that single secret of composition which distinguishes their art from all other art, and which Professor Chamberlain has said it is their special mission to teach to the Occident. Certainly, whoever has once learned to feel the beauty and significance of the old Japanese decorative art can find thereafter little pleasure in the corresponding art of the West. What he has really learned is that Nature's greatest charm is irregularity.

131

Beppu on the Inland Sea

From *Journey by Junk,* copyright, 1953, by Willard Price, reprinted by permission of The John Day Company.

Beppu. . . . is one of the most delightful cities of Japan. Its six hundred hotels and homes of its hundred thousand people are built upon the roof of the infernal regions. Stamp too hard and your foot may go through the thin crust and come out parboiled. The city lies on a mountainside skirting Beppu Bay. Approached by sea, the mountain slopes appear to be stuck with scores of erect white feathers waving in the breeze. These are geysers of steam from the volcanic fires beneath. For this is the city where every house has boiling hot water every minute of the day and night without the cost of a penny for heating, where taps may be left running continually without waste, where bathtubs overflow twelve hours a day and meals are cooked without fuel.

The boiling, grumbling, ever-flowing solfataras of Japan's greatest hot spring resort cover twenty square miles. Hot springs even bubble up through the floor of the bay and have a unique effect upon the fish population. The Black Current which washes the eastern shore of Japan comes from the equator loaded with tropical fish, but most of them soon die in the chilly northern waters. The fortunate ones that happen to be carried into Beppu Bay make themselves quite at home and the waters here are filled with brilliantly-colored immigrants from the South Seas. . . . Even without its hot springs Beppu would qualify as the Japanese Riviera, thanks to a lucky break in climate.

Hot-spring Baths in Hokkaido

From *Year of the Wild Boar, An American Woman in Japan,* copyright, 1942, by Helen Mears, reprinted by permission of J. B. Lippincott Company.

The hot-spring baths were the most delightful part of the trip. The bathrooms were enormous, walled in glass or enclosed with paper panels that were usually open, and they fronted on deep woods or the public highway with equal unconcern. There were often as many as twenty different pools under one roof, the smallest large enough to swim in, and the largest a lake. Not infrequently there would be a half-dozen different sorts of thermal waters under one roof, from simple saline, to sulphur to radioactive.

The fact that these waters had medicinal value and could be used internally as well as externally, had been called to the attention of the Japanese by Western science, but for centuries the hot-springs had been chiefly important as a solution for the problem of running hot water. Since even running cold water is still a luxury for private homes, to have a constant supply of hot water gushing up from the ground is a blessing the Japanese take full advantage of. Hotels and inns use nature's central heating system; the public-baths are built on top of the hot-springs whenever possible; and even private individuals manage to utilize them—the wealthy by building their summer villas near a spring and piping the water into their own bath—the poor by bathing out-of-doors in the lakes and rivers where the hot-springs bubbling up through the water make natural warm pools. Throughout Hokkaido we found such pools.

THE PACIFIC

On the following double-page spread is a photograph of Melbourne as seen from the banks of the Yarra river. It is Australia's second largest city.

Melbourne

From *Australia: Her Heritage, Her Future,* by Paul McGuire, copyright, 1939, by J. B. Lippincott Company, reprinted by permission of J. B. Lippincott Company.

Melbourne is on the River Yarra where it debouches into Port Phillip Bay, an enormous inlet whose ocean entrance is seventy or eighty miles south of Melbourne's seaside suburbs. The city is built much on the square, with streets that cross at right angles, and neat city blocks, and it more resembles (though it may annoy Melbourne to say so) the typical American city than Sydney does. But it has a more settled and decided air than most American cities. It reminds me somewhat of Boston, though Boston would seem a trifle skittish to Melbourne. The business section of the city is north of the Yarra and chiefly about the two long straight streets called Collins and Bourke. Where these are crossed by Elizabeth and Swanston Streets is the heart of the town. Collins and Bourke and the other streets parallel to them have lanes between them, Little Collins Street and Little Bourke Street and so on, and with that perversity common to human nature and traffic, these are naturally the most crowded streets in the city.

South of the Yarra are Melbourne's loudly celebrated gardens and the truly magnificent road that goes down to the beach at St. Kilda; away to the left, Toorak, where opulence resides; and to the right, Port Melbourne, where the liners dock that do not venture into the Yarra.

The Great Barrier Reef

From *From Queensland to the Great Barrier Reef: A Naturalist's Adventures in Australia,* by Noel Monkman, F.R.M.S., reprinted by permission of Angus & Robertson, Ltd., and Doubleday & Company, Inc.

Those brown and purple patches meant coral reefs, and for all their wonder and beauty coral reefs have ripped the bottom from many a stout ship. One of the crew made his way aloft to the cross-trees on the front mast, from where he could plainly see the reefs ahead. The man at the helm watched him intently as the look-out signalled by arm movements the course to take. Dead ahead loomed a great purple patch. The left arm of the look-out man signalled to swing to port. Over went the helm, and the boat swung slowly away from the menace ahead. The right arm now signalled, and the purple patch was left astern. On we went, cautiously threading our way through the labyrinth of reefs until more than two fathoms beneath we could see, through the sparkling clear water, masses of alcyonarian corals spreading their great leathery bulk across the floor of the lagoon. With a rattle, down went the anchor, the engine slowed—stopped—and the boat rode in the lee of an island on the Great Barrier Reef of Australia, the greatest coral formation in the world. The reef extends for more than 1200 miles, and is punctuated with scores of tropic isles which need no romantic glamour of fiction to enhance their charm. Many of these islands are surrounded by coral reefs where wonders of sea life flourish in such profusion that, while one never becomes blasé, the feeling of astonishment is perhaps blunted, and one is apt to accept the almost miraculous as the commonplace.

The Harbor at Sydney

From *Australia and New Zealand,* by Anthony Trollope.

I despair of being able to convey to any reader my own idea of the beauty of Sydney Harbor. I have seen nothing to equal it in the way of land-locked sea scenery,—nothing second to it. Dublin Bay, the Bay of Spezzia, New York, and the Cove of Cork are all picturesquely fine. Bantry Bay, with the marks of sea running up to Glengarrif, is very lovely. But they are not equal to Sydney either in shape, in color, or in variety. I have never seen Naples, or Rio Janeiro, or Lisbon;—but from descriptions and pictures I am led to think that none of them can possess such a world of loveliness of water as lies within Sydney Heads. The proper thing to assert is that the fleets of all the nations might rest securely within the protection of the harbor. How much acreage of sea the fleets of all the nations might require I cannot even surmise;—but if they could be anchored together anywhere, they could surely be anchored at Sydney. . . . I doubt whether I ever read any description of scenery which gave me an idea of the place described, and I am not sure that such effect can be obtained by words. Scott in prose, Byron in verse, are both eloquent in declaring that this or that place is romantic, picturesque, or charming; and their words have been powerful enough to send thousands to see the spots which they have provided. But the charm conveyed has been in the words of the writer, not in the beauty of the place. I know that the task would be hopeless were I to attempt to make others understand the nature of the beauty of Sydney Harbor.

Sydney, the San Francisco of Australia

From *Australia,* by Dr. Charles M. Davis, copyright, 1956, by Nelson Doubleday, Inc., reprinted by permission.

People who think of Australia as a land of sheep raisers are astonished to learn that two out of three Australians are townspeople and that one-half of them live in the six "capital cities." Sydney is the most populous of these; it has one-fifth of the total population of the nation; a million and a half people— as large as Detroit. In the hurry and traffic roar of its Kings Cross a traveler from Piccadilly or 42nd Street would feel right at home. It is the center of Australia's financial life, and a leading producer in such major industries as textiles, automobiles, chemicals, metals, and food processing.

The great Sydney Bridge, the pride of all residents, spans the upper harbor and connects the north shore suburbs with the main city that reaches several miles south to Botany Bay where the international airliners glide to earth. To get around in this sprawling metropolis you have to understand the public transportation system, for there are not nearly enough taxis or "hire cars" to go around. The street cars, "trams," are characteristic and noisy parts of the congested downtown traffic, where they give nostalgic memories to older American visitors.

The Australian

From *Pacific Islands Speaking,* by Armstrong Sperry, copyright ©, 1955, by The Macmillan Company, reprinted by permission of the publisher.

The modern Australian is perhaps the most hospitable man on earth. In many ways it is hard to believe that he is of English descent; he is franker, less reserved, less dignified, more democratic than his forbears. Physically, too, he has evolved into a human being as different from the ordinary Londoner as a mastif from a bulldog. Tall, broad, lean, hard, the Australian is an individual and a tough one. Generations of exposure to the fierce sunlight have even changed the basic color of his skin to a ruddy hue that often borders on bronze. Undoubtedly a part of the modern Australian's fiercely independent spirit is a direct bequest from the ancestry of enterprising pioneers who rebelled against the stuffy atmosphere of Queen Victoria's England.

Tracking Skill of the Australian Native

From *Australian Frontier,* by Ernestine Hill, copyright, 1937, 1942, by Doubleday & Company, Inc., reprinted by permission of Robertson & Mullens, Ltd.

When he is hunting on the plains he can simulate the hopping of a wallaby with uncanny accuracy, stand as still as a tree, or reproduce the cry of a bird to its mate. He is so close to nature that he deceives nature itself. He can track dingoes, the most wary and sensitive of animals, and spear them as they sleep. He can throw a boomerang as no white man, with all his knowledge of mathematics, can do. His delicate hands can "yandy," far more efficiently than any white man's machine.

The skill for which the Australian blackfellow is most famous is tracking. The descendant of generations of hunters, he has a sixth sense and works by pure instinct. The faster he travels, the surer he is of the trail. The slightest change in the blank and inscrutable bushland, whose secrets are hidden from more sophisticated eyes, is easily discerned by him. The native tracks for his daily food and for his safety. He knows by a track whether or not a lizard is fat or thin. He can tell the hoofmarks of wild horses from those of the unshod colts of the station herds and knows how many have passed and what color they were. He can almost tell what mood a passer-by was in, and why, when and where he paused as he traveled that way. He can track over bare rocks and along railroad lines. If he loses the track he circles like a dog and picks it up again. A white man and a native were crossing the wastes of the Territory, far from any beaten trail, in a country of wild tribes, when they came across a boot track. "A white man," said the white man. "No, a half-caste," the native tracker said. The boots that made the track were the standard boots that everyone, white or half-caste, wears out-back on the cattle runs. There was nothing visible in the track to show whether white man or half-caste had left it. But two nights later they came to a water hole and found the half-caste camped there. The tracker could not tell how he knew. If a native is questioned about his methods he becomes uncertain. But left to his instinct he never fails.

Tasmania, Australia's Treasure Island

From *I Travelled a Lonely Land,* by Nina Pulliam, copyright, 1955, used by special permission of the publisher, The Bobbs-Merrill Company, Inc.

Tasmania's said to be the most mountainous island in the world. The mountains are always there, no matter where you look. They're heavily timbered—"enough to last the press of Fleet Street for a hundred years." The little island supplies most of the newsprint used on the mainland and she's now at work enlarging her newsprint manufacturing facilities. . . . .

But it's for her fruit Tasmania is most famous. It's not unusual for the year's crop of apples to run to 8,000,000 or more bushels in the beautiful river valleys of the Huon and the Tamar. And few sights this side of Elysium could be so ethereally lovely as the sight of those wide valleys, white with clouds of pear and apple blossoms in early spring. . . .

As you drive through the gentle foothills, looking across miles of flowering orchards and hop gardens and see the cones of the little oast houses, it's as though you were again in the sublimely beautiful Kentish hills of England in springtime. The storybook villages are tied together by lazy roads winding through the green valleys, where sheep graze passively and big Clydesdale horses help turn the soil. You clatter over the cobble streets of one little township or another and run along the gravelly roads between, perhaps inching your way through a mob of heavy-coated sheep which, like you, use the highway as their thoroughfare. They'll likely be attended by a white-haired ancient, a small boy and a brisk and busy little sheep dog.

The fragrance of the pear trees wafts across the road, the riotous gorse turns the land to gold and green. It might be Ireland or it might be England. Wherever it is, it's beautiful and peaceful, like a place through which you strolled in a dream you had of a long-lost spring.

Topsy-Turvy Land

From *Adventure,* copyright, 1931, by Carveth Wells, reprinted by permission.

Australia. . . . is a continent bigger than the United States. . . . The country itself, as well as the animals, birds and plants is topsy-turvy. Rivers, for instance, instead of rising in the interior and running into the sea, rise on the sea coast and run inland to disappear altogether. Australian trees instead of shedding their leaves, shed their bark and the leaves remain on the tree. Australia is also the home of the duck-billed platypus, that extraordinary freak of nature which has a head like a duck, lays eggs and suckles its young.

Some Australian birds have no wings, others laugh uproariously, and another species attacks sheep and eats their kidneys. One of the most interesting Australian birds builds a large mound of rubbish and deposits its eggs in the mound. There they hatch without any further attention on the part of the female. . . . Australia is the home of several kinds of kangaroos including some that live in trees, their babies when born being the size of a small walnut!

Beauty of New Zealand

From *Pacific Islands Speaking,* by Armstrong Sperry, copyright ©, 1955, by The Macmillan Company, reprinted by permission of the publisher.

Like the Frenchman who, when asked why his compatriots were such reluctant travelers, replied: "Why should anyone want to leave France?" the New Zealander answers the same question about his own country: "Where would we go to find anything more beautiful than New Zealand?"

And it would indeed be difficult to discover a greater variety of natural beauty than the two islands have to offer. In area they are about the size of Colorado. At the northern end of North Island one finds blazing tropical beaches whose waters are the home of out-sized swordfish and marlin. One moves south through sub-tropical forests dominated by the famed *kauri* pines which, like our redwoods, are of immense age and size. The center of North Island is one of the earth's safety valves, where volcanoes erupt through vents in the earth's crust. Rotorua, with its boiling mud and steaming geysers, rivals Yellowstone Park. It is in this region that many of the native Maoris live, and they make ingenious use of the natural steam cauldrons in preparing their food.

Across Cook strait—the point from which the great James Cook discovered that New Zealand was made up of two separate islands—lies South Island. This is country of spectacular beauty. The 12,300-foot heights of Mount Cook, perpetually covered with snow, reach icy fingers of land down into the sea. Here too are the "Southern Alps"—great chains of glaciated peaks, reflected in the mirror-like surface of innumerable lakes.

Auckland, the Queen City

From *New Zealand Now,* by Oliver Duff, reprinted by permission of the author.

Auckland is not what it is just because its citizens are what they are. It is not the Queen City because two hundred thousand people keep on saying so. It has left Wellington, Christchurch, and Dunedin behind because it lies degrees nearer to the Equator; because it has always had land for the people to build their houses and water in which to swing their ships; because it is in the tract of trade to Australia, the first port of call from America, and the nearest point for trade with what we still foolishly call the South Seas and the Far East. Timber has helped it, gold, coal, sugar, and gum. But nothing means so much to it today as butter, cheese, and milk. It is a rich garden fertilised from the cowshed. And because cows are the foundation of its economy, the grocer, the butcher, the draper, and the baker are the guiding stars of its municipal life. . . . It has the short-circuited economy of the dairy farm itself—grass today, cream tomorrow, and your cheque at the end of the month. It has of course many rich men, but most of them have become rich in trade, which means exchange, and keeping things moving, and *not* having too many poor men. Auckland is a prosperous city—prosperous rather than comfortable. It moves, its pots keep on boiling; however full they are, they are not pushed to one side of the stove.

Pageant of History

From *New Zealand,* by James A. Michener, reprinted by special permission from *Holiday,* copyright, 1951, by The Curtis Publishing Company.

There is one aspect of Maori culture that is sheer delight, one of those perfect art forms that haunt the memory with true loveliness. Young Maori girls, dressed in knotted cord blouses and skirts made of flax stems, become adept in swinging poi balls, made of compressed rushes tied to strings. (Short poi, six-inch strings; long poi, eighteen-inch.) In delicate rhythms, sometimes brushing their skirts so as to yield an extra beat, teams of girls execute prolonged and intricate drills.

On festive days they do the canoe poi. Then, with each girl whirling two short poi, they seat themselves upon the ground so as to represent their tribal canoe. In back of them a chief rushes up and down flourishing a green-stone club and urging them on. Somewhere in the shadows an old woman stands, chanting through blue-tattooed lips some wild Polynesian account of the great migration. Now, in their canoe, the girls make the poi balls fly. At first it seems nothing, merely another dance. Then slowly the poi take on the rhythm of the sea. Shoulders begin to weave as if hands carried great paddles. The chief rants and cries. Always the mournful woman chants in her husky voice.

Now the poi balls whir in the air, striking beaded skirts, tapping against the body. The entire audience is sailing in that ancestral canoe and the night is tense with the sound of the poi balls. Suddenly the woman moans. In silence the girls fall backward, as their ancestors had once collapsed from near starvation. There is now no sound but that of the mysterious poi balls, echoing the tiny slap of waves against the historic canoe. Then the chief shouts. The old woman screams the last measure of the chant. The girls revive, and the trembling poi balls leap to a beat of joy. And there is no one who cannot see that early vision of The Long White Cloud!

On the following double-page spread is a photograph of the island of Kauai, "garden of Hawaii," the oldest and fourth in size in the Hawaiian chain.

KRONFELD © PAA

Kauai

Kauai. . . is known popularly as "The Garden Isle." The reason is not far to seek. There are miles of flowering trees and vines, waving cane fields, rich paddies, and vast pineapple plantations. From the tops of cliffs, waterfalls trail like mists that are shot with rainbows.

Waimea Canyon with its red-hued rain-eroded walls, is a miniature Grand Canyon. Here the bustling commotion of Honolulu or Hilo seems a thousand miles away. . . . It is an unforgettable experience to walk along Kauai's famous barking sands. Actually a footstep causes the sand to bark like a dog! One explanation is that as the grains of sand dry out after being soaked with rain or sea, they acquire a film of condensed gases which vibrate resonantly under pressure.

On Kauai there is an ancient series of irrigation ditches which, according to legend, were built by a race of dwarfs known to the Hawaiians as Memehunes. Scientists scoff at the idea; but whatever the origin of the ditches, the squared-off blocks of rock are marvelously fitted together, without cement, in a stone craftsmanship never possessed by the Hawaiians themselves.

Night in Honolulu

Night in Honolulu is soft and furry and mysterious, despite the glow of neon, the hum of motors, the voices, and the trampling of feet on paved streets. The familiar scene takes on an altered aspect, scented delicately with fragrances of flowers and fruit and the salty breath of the sea. Footfalls of half-forgotten gods move through the velvet shadows where the waves lap lightly against the modern piers. Harbor lights wink rhythmically on and off, like some endlessly repeated message in code. Shafts of yellow radiance fan out across the water from freighters moored in Kapalama Basin; rows of portholes gleam from the liner that lies at the foot of Fort Street. The masts of the schooner-yacht that arrived lately from the deeper-south sea rise dark against the sky. Off to the left, where the reef curves past the crouching bulk of Diamond Head, flare the torches of fishermen. And far out, rising and falling and winking out behind the swells, the little, lonely lamps of belated sampans twinkle between the twin vastnesses of sea and sky.

Somewhere a song wails into the night, weaving a somber melody around the muttering throb of strings; the syllables fall petal soft in the round Hawaiian tongue. And you feel again that catch in the throat, that burning behind the eyelids, that quickening of heart and breath. You laugh at yourself for it, reminding yourself that all this is just so much romantic nonsense. But it gets you, just the same.

Vacationers' Paradise

From *Our Hawaii,* by Erna Fergusson, copyright, 1942, by Alfred A. Knopf, Inc., reprinted by permission.

Waikiki's narrow crescent beach, growing narrower every year, faces southwest. It begins below Diamond Head, a dead volcanic crater, weathering starkly down into gullies of rock and sand, and making its own face arid by forcing the trade winds to round its flank and descend on Honolulu obliquely. Its cactus-growth stoniness never relents; it holds a fort in its uplifted cup, and even when it throws back the sunset light Diamond Head remains as adamant as its name. . . . The arc of the shore and the ships on the horizon make a frame. Palms and lesser growth along the shore give it a green mat. And the picture —at least for one's first few days in Honolulu—is the sparkling splendor of the sea.

When I first saw it before ten o'clock in the morning it was milky green in the breakers. Beyond swelling rollers lifted swatches of lavender and lilac as though flowers floated just under the water's surface. Farther out it deepened into clear jade where bobbing black dots marked swimmers. And against the horizon lay a heavier stream of lapis lazuli. It was, they told me, rather a dull morning. But it was as much iridescence as I could have stood for a first dose, especially as all the color notes were set in the silver filigree of foaming wave crests. Then a breeze came ruffling along crosswise and turned my milky absinthe frappe into sharp clear emerald. I sent my bags upstairs, chose a comfortable swing, and settled down to watching the surf-boarders.

On the following double-page spread is a photograph of Cook's Bay, Tahiti, forever a symbol of idyllic existence in the dreams of men.

KRONFELD © PAA

Tahiti

From *Voyage to the Amorous Islands,* by Newton A. Rowe, reprinted by permission of Essential Books, Inc., and Andre Deutsch Limited.

The hour-glass-shaped island of Tahiti—roughly half-way between the north of New Zealand and Panama—is about a hundred and twenty-five miles in circumference. It consists of two peninsulas, one about ninety miles in circumference and nearly circular, the other about thirty miles in circumference, oval shaped and connected by a low isthmus about a couple of miles across. . . . The larger peninsula is called by the natives Great Tahiti of the Golden Haze. The smaller one is Little Tahiti, or Disturbed Sea.

With cliffs where it is not palm-fringed, forest-clad, wasp-waisted and mountainous, the island has a peculiar clarity of atmosphere. There is something soft and voluptuous about the light, a fact noticed not only by artists but by the natives, for there is much of the artist in them. A curious shimmering magic seems to hang over the sharply towering mountains with their forests, their lawn-like patches of fern and bamboo, their headlong waterfalls, about the foaming coral reefs and the pellucid lagoons.

Coming in to Papeete

From *Mystic Isles of the South Seas,* by Frederick O'Brien, copyright, 1921, by Appleton-Century-Crofts, Inc., reprinted by permission of the publisher.

Greener than the Barbadoes, like malachite upon the dazzling Spanish Main, Tahiti gleamed as a promise of Elysium.

A lighthouse, tall minister of warning, lifted upon a headland, and suddenly there was disclosed intimately the brilliant, shimmering surf breaking on the tortuous coral reef that banded the island a mile away. It was like a circlet of quicksilver in the sun, a quivering, shining, waving wreath. Soon we heard the eternal diapason of these shores, the constant and immortal music of the breakers on the white stone barrier, a low, deep, resonant note that lulls the soul to sleep by day as it does the body by night. . . .

A stretch of houses showed—the warehouses and shops of the merchants along the beach, the spire of a church, a line of wharf, a hundred tiny homes all but hidden in the foliage of the ferns. These gradually came into view as the ship, after skirting along the reef, steered through a break in the foam, a pass in the treacherous coral, and glided through opalescent and glassy shallows to a quay where all Papeete waited to greet us. The quay was filled with women and men and children and dogs. . . . Conspicuous above all were the Tahitian and part-Tahitian girls. In their long, graceful, waistless tunics of brilliant hues, their woven bamboo or pandanus hats, decorated with fresh flowers, their feet bare or thrust into French slippers, their brown eyes shining with yearning, they were so many Circes to us from the sea.

. . . Cries rang out in French, in Tahitian and in English. Islanders, returning, demanded information as to health, business ventures, happenings. Merry laughter echoed from the roof of the great shed, and I felt my heart suddenly become joyous.

A <u>Bal</u> in Tahiti

From *Rainbow in Tahiti,* copyright, 1948, by Caroline Guild, reprinted by permission.

The young people were there and everyone else regardless of age, from the dignified old Queen to nursing babies. And under every table, set out on an open terrace, lay at least one dog. The bolder hounds joined the dancers from time to time, bringing more than one couple sprawling to the floor. The dance was held in a big barren hall, temporarily transformed into a garden. The ugly walls were blanketed with green leaves of coconut palms and flowers. A bar from which a river of champagne flowed extended the length of the hall. Popping of corks mingling with the yelps of trodden dogs punctuated the music made by a profusely perspiring orchestra. The powder room for the *tanes* was to the left of the entrance in the shade of a mango tree. A clump of bushes on the right provided a secluded squatting place for the *vahines.*

There seemed to be no social barriers so far as color was concerned. I saw every shade from the typically white skin of a woman recently from Paris to the deep café-au-lait of Polynesians. Actually, the "first families" were half-castes, results of unions, churched or otherwise, between Tahitian maidens and the first white men to stop here from whaling ships and men-of-war. Men came to the dance with their wives or with their mistresses—occasionally both. Wives and mistresses were equally busy for a few days previous running up dresses on their sewing machines. There was no place to buy ready-made clothes in Papeete but that does not mean there was no chic. With French blood predominating, Paris dictating, and competition accelerating them, the local belles were a sight for the eye.

Morning in Samoa

From *Coming of Age in Samoa,* by Margaret Mead, copyright, 1928, by William Morrow & Company, Inc., copyright renewed, 1956, by Margaret Mead, reprinted by permission of the publisher.

The life of the day begins at dawn, or if the moon has shown until daylight, the shouts of the young men may be heard before dawn from the hillside. Uneasy in the night, populous with ghosts, they shout lustily to one another as they hasten with their work. As the dawn begins to fall among the soft brown roofs and the slender palm trees stand out against a colorless, gleaming sea, lovers slip home from trysts beneath the palm trees or in the shadow of beached canoes, that the light may find each sleeper in his appointed place. Cocks crow, negligently, and a shrill-voiced bird cries from the breadfruit trees. The insistent roar of the reef seems muted to an undertone for the sounds of a waking village. Babies cry, a few short wails before sleepy mothers give them the breast. Restless little children roll out of their sheets and wander drowsily down to the beach to freshen their faces in the sea. Boys, bent upon an early fishing, start collecting their tackle and go to rouse their more laggard companions. Fires are lit, here and there, the white smoke hardly visible against the paleness of the dawn. The whole village, sheeted and frowsy, stirs, rubs its eyes, and stumbles towards the beach.

Along the Coasts of Samoa

From *Reminiscences of the South Seas,* by John La-Farge, copyright, 1912, by Doubleday & Company, Inc., reprinted by permission.

Two mornings ago we left Vaiala, and rowed westward within the reefs, along the north coast of our island of Upolu. . . . There was all the charm that belongs to the near coasting of land in smooth waters: the rise and fall of the great green reflections in the blue satin of the sea inside of the reef; the sharp blue outside of the white line of reef all iridescent with the breaking of the surf; the patches of coral, white or yellow or purple, wavering below the crystal swell, so transparent as to recall the texture of uncut topaz or amethyst; the shoals of brilliant fish, blue and gold-green, as bright and flickering as tropical hummingbirds; the contrast of great shadows upon the mountain, black with an inkiness that I have never seen elsewhere; the fringes of golden or green palms upon the shores, sometimes inviting, sometimes dreary. And our rowers in their brightest waist cloths, with great backs and arms and legs, red and glistening in the sun that wet them even as much as the cocoanut oil with which they were anointed. . . .

Still, beauty of nature, and plenty of soft air do not prevent fatigue, even if they soothe it, and I was glad when in the afternoon we had reached Leulu-moenga—our final halt—a village type of Samoa, spread all over the sandy flat of the back beach, and half hidden in trees.

Party on Samoa

From *Our Samoan Adventure,* by Fanny and Robert Louis Stevenson, and edited by Charles Neider, copyright, 1955, by Charles Neider ©, reprinted by permission of Harper & Brothers.

Tuesday, 12th September, 1893: Yesterday was perhaps the brightest in the annals of Vailima. I got leave from Captain Bickford to have the band of the *Katoomba* come up, and they came, fourteen of 'em, with drum, fife, cymbals, and bugles, blue jackets, white caps, and smiling faces. The house was all decorated with scented greenery above and below. We had not only our own nine out-door workers but a contract party that we took on in charity to pay their war-fine; the band besides, as it came up the mountain, had collected a following of children by the way, and we had a picking of Samoan ladies to receive them. Chicken, ham, cake, and fruits were served out with coffee and lemonade, and all the afternoon we had rounds of claret negus, flavored with rum and limes. They played to us, they danced, they sang, they tumbled. Our boys came in the end of the verandah and gave *them* a dance for a while. It was anxious work getting this stopped once it had begun, but I knew the band was going on a programme. Finally they gave three cheers for Mr. and Mrs. Stevenson, shook hands, formed up and marched off playing—till a kicking horse in the paddock put their pipes out something of the suddenest—we thought the big drum was gone, but Simile flew to the rescue. And so they wound away down the hill with ever another call of the bugle, leaving us extinct with fatigue, but perhaps the most contented hosts that ever watched the departure of successful guests.

Our Samoan House

From *Adventures in Paradise,* copyright ©, 1955, by Willard Price, reprinted by permission of The John Day Company.

Our house is one room only and quite innocent of walls. Sitting in it, you may enjoy a complete panoramic view of sea and shore, village and forest, merely by turning your head.

The house is built upon a coral platform four feet above the ground. This improves our view—it also makes it easier for the village to keep an eye on us. Of course we are under constant observation, but that is only fair; we observe others just as closely. There is scarcely an hour of the day or night when two or three persons are not standing below the edge of the platform, looking in, or comfortably seated on the mats inside the house so that they may be on hand in case we need their help. . . .

But it is impossible not to enjoy the clean open effect, the freedom from clutter of this simple house, the feel of outdoor living, the fresh sea air, the visits of birds and butterflies who make themselves at home in the rafters, the unobstructed view in all directions. It's a pleasure just to lie on your back and admire the intricate construction of the roof interior with its hundreds of breadfruit ribs stitched in place with sennit and overlaid with sugarcane thatch. The workmanship is neat and trim to the last degree, and as artistic as a beautifully made basket. Housebuilding is not left to amateurs. It is a highly skilled trade passed from father to son over many generations. Carpenters rank with pastors and chiefs in public respect.

South Sea Fishing

From *The Cruise of the Snark,* by Jack London. Permission granted by Irving Shepard, copyright owner.

There was the fishing. One did not have to go in search of it, for it was there at the rail. A three-inch steel hook, on the end of a stout line, with a piece of white rag for bait, was all that was necessary to catch bonitas weighing from ten to twenty-five pounds. Bonitas feed on flying-fish, wherefore they are unaccustomed to nibbling at the hook. They strike as gamely as the gamest fish in the sea, and their first run is something that no man who has ever caught them will forget. Also, bonitas are the veriest cannibals. The instant one is hooked he is attacked by his fellows. Often and often we hauled them on board with fresh, clean-bitten holes in them the size of teacups.

One school of bonitas, numbering many thousands, stayed with us day and night for more than three weeks. Aided by the *Snark,* it was great hunting; for they cut a swath of destruction through the ocean half a mile wide and fifteen hundred miles in length. They ranged along abreast of the *Snark* on either side, pouncing upon the flying-fish her forefoot scared up. Since they were continually pursuing astern the flying-fish that survived for several flights, they were always overtaking the *Snark,* and at any time one could glance astern and on the front of a breaking wave see scores of their silvery forms coasting down just under the surface.

Fijian Stage Setting

From *Fiji,* by James A. Michener, reprinted by special permission from *Holiday,* copyright, 1950, by The Curtis Publishing Company.

There are few places more pleasant to visit than Fiji. It consists of some thirty main islands, of which two predominate. The largest is Viti Levu—4053 square miles—about half the size of New Jersey. The western half of this tropical island always surprises Americans, for it resembles Wyoming. Red hills, sweeping plateaus, and outcropping mountains make it surprisingly beautiful.

Along the shore line one gets a slight feeling of the tropics, since palms flourish here. This is where the sugar cane is grown, and the visitor to an island often described as primitive is astonished to find a railroad crossing and re-crossing the highway. Along it small steel cradles move the rich cane to the C.S.R. factories. Then suddenly, almost mysteriously, at about the middle of Viti Levu, the climate, rainfall, vegetation, and terrain change abruptly and one is no longer in dry Wyoming but in a teeming tropical jungle. Rain clouds, driven by the trade winds from the east, drop their moisture as they hit the central mountains. Rivers that look like tired dishwater wind heavily laden to the sea. Jungle plants crowd the road. Mist and storm engulf the land for days on end, and the rainfall is sometimes prodigious. Yet the jungle is beautiful, for flowers and strange trees abound. Most of the population lives in this rainy sector. Small fields are cleared and planted with dalo (called taro on other islands). Vegetables grow luxuriantly and there are huge banana plantations. The land is rich and productive.

Suva

From *A Writer's Note-book,* copyright, 1949, by W. Somerset Maugham, reprinted by permission of Doubleday & Company, Inc., the author, and Messrs. Heinemann.

The bay is fine and spacious, surrounded by grey hills that stretch away mysteriously into a blue distance. You feel that in that farther country, thickly wooded, there is a strange and secret life. It suggests something aboriginal and darkly cruel. The town stretches along the borders of the harbor. Here are many frame buildings, more shops than at Apia, but there is still the air of the trading station which the place must once have been. The natives walk about in lava-lavas and singlets or shirts, tall strapping men for the most part, as dark as Negroes, with their curly hair, often bleached with lime, cut into a curious shape. There are numbers of Hindus, walking softly, dressed in white; and the women wear nose-rings, gold chains round their necks and bangles on their arms. When you go out into the country you pass crowded villages of Hindus and everywhere you see them working in the fields. They wear nothing but a loincloth and their bodies are frighteningly thin. The country is subtropical, palm trees grow poorly, but there are great groves of mangoes; it has not the blitheness of Samoa, it is more sombre and the green is heavy and dark. The air is hot and oppressive, heavy too, and the rain beats down incessantly.

THE AMERICAS

On the following double-page spread is a photograph of Wonder Lake in Mount McKinley National Park, Alaska. Mount McKinley rises majestically to 20,270 feet.

Mount McKinley National Park

From *The Real Book About Our National Parks,* by Nelson Beecher Keyes, copyright ©, 1957, by Doubleday & Company, Inc., reprinted by permission.

The highest point on the North American Continent is a large mountain peak about 250 miles below the Arctic Circle in south-central Alaska. The Indians called it *Denali,* "home of the sun," and they claimed it was the enormous rock hurled by one of their gods at his wife who was attempting to run away. It was 1902 before white men set foot upon its ponderous slopes, and 1910 before they had made their way to the summit of this 20,270-foot giant, named McKinley for our twenty-fifth president, who was assassinated in 1901. As they came to know this majestic mountain better, they at last realized that it was actually the loftiest peak above its base in the world. It towers some 17,000 feet above the broad plateau on its north and west sides. . . .

Here stood a great natural scenic wonder, which deserved to be kept safe and unspoiled for the enjoyment of future generations. So, in 1917, it was established as the thirteenth of our national parks by an act of Congress. Five years later it was expanded to cover an area of 2645 square miles, while further extensions to the north and east in 1932 brought it up to 1,939,493 acres. It is thus the second largest of our parks, exceeded only by Yellowstone.

A Breath-Taking Mob of Seals

From *U. S. A.—Untamed Alaska,* by William L. Worden, in *Holiday,* copyright, 1953, by The Curtis Publishing Company, reprinted by permission of Brandt & Brandt.

From the air, the seal herds were black masses, undulating smooth backs covering nearly a dozen rookeries, each occupying a huge, black sand beach. From the land, the seals are first a great sound, then a massive odor and finally, as the visitor peers from a headland or cautiously makes his way along a catwalk strung twenty feet above the brawling mass, a breath-taking mob. A hundred thousand pairs of round eyes turn to look at him. Ten thousand bull voices roar warnings to harems and multitudinous offspring or defiance to the intruder. A hundred bulls, each weighing close to a thousand pounds, bare their teeth and move ponderously toward him. The visitor resists an impulse to run away, and then leaps half out of his skin as still another pair of round eyes, at first curious and then terrified, stares up from some crevice almost at his feet—and a seal puppy, yelping in terror, races madly away.

This is the seal herd—thousands upon thousands—swimming, fighting, eating, feeding their young. The bulls charge or stand, depending on the time of year; and the cows stand or run, depending on what protection their lords provide. Seals jump twenty feet down from rock to rock, plunge into the sea, or flee, clambering over each other, as men approach. Sounds of their fear and hatred swell to an ear-shattering roar. It may be minutes before the visitor notices the rocks. These are huge boulders left over from some natural cataclysm, but all have been worn smooth by thousands of years of seal occupancy.

The Great Land

From *A Guide to Alaska,* by Merle Colby, copyright, 1939, by The Macmillan Company, reprinted by permission of the publishers.

It is a common American belief that Alaska is largely covered with ice and inhabited by Eskimos who live in ice houses and drink blubber. Alaska, the Great Land of the Aleuts, the Brobdingnag of Gulliver, does contain a great deal of ice—in its warmer regions. The glacier system of the Mt. St. Elias range is the largest ice field in the world outside the Polar caps. But this country also contains the largest chain of volcanoes in the world and the highest mountain in the world, measured from base to peak, and most of Alaska lies north of the glacier ice. Flowers and berries grow profusely in this country. Delphiniums are nine feet high, strawberries are two inches in diameter, and cabbages weigh fifty pounds. Alaska streams are the spawning ground of the Pacific salmon, Alaska seas contain furs and foodstuffs, shrimp and whales. Lemuel Gulliver quite lost his perspective here, and it is not surprising that average American citizens have mistaken notions about the Territory.

Alaska's Famous Bears

From *Alaska's Animals and Fishes,* copyright, 1956, by Frank Dufresne, reprinted by permission of A. S. Barnes and Company, Inc.

On all the earth there is nothing to compare with Alaska's assortment of bruins. It comprises many species and subspecies ranging in color from the cream-colored Toklat Grizzly of the Alaska Range to the almost coal-black Shiras Bear of Admiralty Island, and in size from the small Alaska Grizzly of Norton Sound to the giant Kodiak Brown Bear. Admiralty Island, alone, with a bear population of almost one to each of its 1,600 square miles, has been credited with four grizzlies and one brown bear species. Other sections of the Territory present nearly as puzzling an array of these great beasts. The layman stands awed by their numbers and size, confused by their variety. . . .

To see the typical Alaska Grizzly one should go to the high slopes of the Alaska Range. Along the receding snowline in June the mother with her faded straw-colored coat ambles from gulch to ridge, digs out ground squirrels with much huffing and puffing, and casting them before her dark-colored cubs, incites them to squeals and bickerings. By way of variety she grubs a few roots, crops a patch of grass tips, until, giving in to the persistent fretting of her cubs she will sprawl back against a hummock to let them nurse their fill. In another part of the range a mother of the previous year has taken a mate for the June-July honeymoon period. High in the crags a lone male hurls himself out onto a snow-filled gully and comes sliding down the mountain as though riding a bobsled.

Not alone because of their formidable proportions do the grizzly and brown bears of Alaska command respect. Often enough to maintain this respect they will become the hunter rather than the hunted. Mothers with cubs will sometimes attack; wounded bears fight back with unbridled ferocity.

Metropolis of the North

From *Alaska,* by Dr. David W. Lantis, copyright, 1957, by Nelson Doubleday, Inc., reprinted by permission.

Anchorage, metropolis of Alaska, is one of the Territory's newer towns and also its best planned. Created as the administrative center for the Alaska Railroad in 1915, Anchorage has changed from a tent village into a cosmopolitan city with nearly 30,000 inhabitants, daily newspaper, and television stations. Many thousands of flights annually move from its new International Airport; in fact it ranks among the top ten cities of the continent in volume of air traffic.

Anchorage does not suffer from the shortage of flat land that constricts some of the larger Alaska towns. It is a spreadout community with a rectangular street plan. Fourth Avenue, its busy main street, has several small skyscrapers, and in the evening blazes with neon signs. Its diversified sources of income include railroad business, military installations, coal fields, gold mines, and the trade of the Territory's leading agricultural area, the Matanuska Valley. The government chose its site well in establishing, in 1935, the resettlement project in the Matanuska Valley. Today, although most of the original families are gone, more than 10,000 acres are under cultivation in the fertile, wooded land. Clearing here, as elsewhere, is slow; if it is done under contract by bulldozer, the cost is around $200 an acre. The Valley's dairy products and vegetables help to feed Anchorage and the surrounding military bases.

Flying Over Alaska

From *It's All Adventure,* copyright, 1938, by Peter Freuchen, reprinted by permission of Rinehart & Company, Incorporated.

Flying over Alaska was a magnificent experience. Beneath us as we took off from Anchorage lay Cook Inlet, deceptively calm and smooth from the air. In that stretch of water there is a difference of 27 feet between high and low tide, and at noon it looks entirely unlike its appearance early in the morning. But the highest tides conceivable make no difference to an airplane, and we crossed it swiftly to find ourselves above an extensive forest. It seemed to me that the trees looked spindling and weak, and here and there were stretches where they had died and bleached to withered skeletons of gray. The remorseless tundra was creeping in upon those trees, sapping their vitality as it saps the vigor of everything that tries to live upon it, whether men, animals, or plants.

Smaller and smaller grew the forest, the heights of the trees diminishing from minute to minute as we flashed over them, until at last there was nothing beneath us but the bare expanse of the pure tundra, without a sign of life....

Closer and closer drew the huge mass of Mount McKinley, the highest peak in Alaska, and beneath us the land began to rise steadily. Rivers brown with mud tumbled down toward the flatlands behind us, gradually dwindling to mere mountain streams. Then we were winging along over the Alaska Range, with the peaks towering up so abruptly that I had the feeling they were leaping to snatch at our plane.

McGill University

From *Montreal: Seaport and City,* copyright, 1942, by Stephen Leacock, reprinted by permission of Doubleday & Company, Inc.

The grounds of McGill University are beautifully situated in what is, in a sense, the center of Montreal, the slope at the base of the mountain running straight down toward the river. Unlike many colleges buried in commercial cities, it has the great advantage that it can be seen all at once; not really all of it, but enough to give the finished picture of a college and a campus, the oldest building, of the greatest dignity, recognizable at once as such at the top of the slope. The newer buildings, magnificent in size, frame the sides of the campus. All the central open space is a playground dotted with great trees, pierced with a central avenue of tall elms and maples, running up through the beautiful Roddick Gates from Sherbrooke Street below. The trees verge already on a hundred years of age. The photographs of past days show them as slender little saplings when all Montreal made merry at the visit of the gay young Prince of Wales in 1860. The old building at the top is the Arts Building, battered, renewed, built over, pinned under, having lost everything but its beauty. Again and again common sense whispered, "Knock it down; build it like Pittsburgh, fifty stories high . . . stick elevators into it to make it like Columbia. This thing begins to look like those old places in Oxford." But no one ever dared to. It was the old dilemma, the old problem as between affection and change, continuity or a new start. So there it stays.

Quebec

From *Quebec: Portrait of a Province,* by Blowden Davies, reprinted by permission of William Heinemann, Ltd., Toronto.

Among all the cities of North America, none has achieved a more distinctive character than the old fortress city of Quebec. Even the high tides of tourists cannot entirely erase its natural serenity. All too many go to Quebec only in July and August; the wise will plan their visits to the old city at other times, when spring, delicate and yet exuberant, lies like a lustre over the city and its environment, or when autumn flows like molten gold over the countryside. Or even when snow adds the final touch of enchantment to the St. Lawrence Valley.

It is in these quiet seasons that the real Quebec reveals itself, as the people of the city go about their accustomed ways of life, unconscious of the visitor . . . . The romantic city of the past is still there—half stone, half shadow— and those who will may still sense the presence of friendly spirits who walk abroad in the legend-haunted streets. Another life still moves on in old Quebec, half-remembered—a generation that goes about its ghostly business in cuirass and gauntlet, in powdered wigs and high red heels.

Perhaps it is because Quebec is so many-faceted that it preserves its charm. . . . It is a dreamy city of the past, living on memories and legends, and it is a modern capital, involved in the problems of its own restless age.

On the Gaspé

From *Away to the Gaspé,* by Gordon Brinley, copyright ©, 1935, by Dodd, Mead and Company, Inc., reprinted by permission of the publisher.

There lay Percé! On the last green slopes of towering mountains facing blue waters and its own stupendous miracle, the Pierced Rock. . . .

Up against the western sky, on our left, rose ancient Mt. Ste. Anne, shouldering Rosy Peak; and locking hands in a swing toward the north, the cliffs of Three Sisters and Cap Barrè. At the feet of these cliffs a beach curved back south, past the undulations of Mt. Joli (on which the buildings of a hotel stood) and Mt. Logan, continuing south, passing us to the right, and so on to the unseen Bay of Chaleurs. Within the embrace of these mountains and beaches lay land possibly a quarter of a mile wide at its greatest depth. On its green acres, swept now with the white of daisies, were scattered houses and farm buildings. A handsome stone Catholic church marked the northern, and a charming little English church the southern reaches of the community. Along its one main street, and its half dozen intersecting lanes clustered the homes and hotels and shops that to travelers like ourselves make up this county seat of Percé.

Vancouver

From *The Ports of British Columbia,* by Agnes Rothery, copyright, 1943, by Agnes Rothery Pratt, reprinted by permission of Doubleday & Company, Inc.

Mountains—with their peaks and crests and tumbled masses leaping down into the water. A harbor—a hundred miles around its edge, completely surrounded by those mountains, save at the Narrows, where an airy, single-span bridge completes the frame. And up and down the slopes, along the shore looking over the deep, protected water, Vancouver—one of the most superbly situated cities on the globe. Rejoicing as a strong man to run a race, Vancouver is posed upon an incomparable vantage ground.

At its back crowd and press the resources of all Canada, with railroads bringing them to its feet. Before its face beckons the Orient, which must be in the future, as it has been in the past, its direct and omnivorous customer. Into its outstretched right hand and into its left pour the riches of British Columbia: riches from the forests above the ground and mines below the ground; riches from the sea and all that in it is. . . . Vancouver . . . has skyscrapers, airports, shipyards, docks, piers, and warehouses, industrial plants, storage plants, and grain elevators; although it is the third-largest city in Canada, it has hardly more than rubbed its eyes, yawned, stretched, and considered the racecourse. Vancouver is an infant among cities. . . . British Columbia regards its chief metropolis with pride. In fact, almost half of the population of the province chooses to live within a twenty-five-mile radius of it.

Toronto

From *Ontario,* by Marjorie Wilkins Campbell, copyright, Canada, 1953, by The Ryerson Press, reprinted by permission of the publisher.

It was late September, and warm. An autumn haze glowed about the brown bulk of the Parliament Buildings. The tall structures downtown wore a landscaped look. The soaring TV aerial of the Canadian Broadcasting Corporation on Jarvis Street suggested the Eiffel Tower in a park. Houses, churches, university buildings nestled among the trees far below. You could scarcely see the city for the trees. Maples, still green, and old chestnuts, and tawny oaks recalling the days when the site of the Park Plaza was covered with bush. An observant stranger, Malcolm MacDonald, on his first visit, called Toronto "a million people living in a forest."

The Park Plaza is at Toronto's main crossroads. North and south the traffic flows along University Avenue and Avenue Road, from the waterfront to the faroff suburbs. East and west the stream of cars and trucks and red street cars speed along Bloor Street, which leads to the historic Danforth Road on the east and the equally historic Dundas Road on the west. . . . Bloor Street, Toronto's Park Avenue, was crowded that lovely September afternoon. Many a woman has come up from New York to buy an ermine jacket, an English suit or diamonds at its many smart shops.

On the following page is a photograph of the New York skyline viewed from the east at night. The dramatic building in the center is the United Nations headquarters.

KRONFELD © PAA

Hope for Man's Ultimate Realization of Peace

New York's population has increased ten thousand-fold since the first City Fathers were named in 1653. To these eight millions, and to the millions more who visit it, or see pictures of it, or read of it, what does this aggregate of stone and steel, this city which has become the world's first, mean? . . .

Moving among New York's slums, you could weep for the poor who dwell in them except that you know that hundreds will struggle up, one day, to the richest mansions on Park Avenue and to the quiet dignity of Sutton Place. You will find comfort in the thought that wiser City Fathers are aware of the tragedies that grow out of the slums, and that they have built or sponsored the building of cleaner and better housing centers.

Standing off from the city in the Brooklyn and Staten Island ferries, or coming in from the sea, your eyes will widen and your heart will soften at what the rising sun does to the soaring towers that look down on the spot where the first Dutch settlers built. Then the eye picks out the cluster of new United Nations buildings, a ghostly group on East River shore at midtown, and sudden warmth comes aflame inside. You think that this glittering island, grown from wilderness to great metropolis in three hundred years, holds that one hope for man's ultimate realization of peace—reason enough for the existence of New York, even if there were no other.

Statue of Liberty

On October 28, 1886, the Statue of Liberty was unveiled on Bedloe's Island in the Bay. Like the Hudson River and the Palisades, it is now accepted as one of the natural glories of New York. We who are used to it seldom see it consciously, but it is in our souls and governs our attitude toward the contemporary world. It is a work of art beyond criticism now, for no one knows how deeply it has penetrated into the life of America and of the world, nor how much it has strengthened the ideal of liberty by standing there year after year and holding a lighted torch in the sky. The Constitution is no more explicit than this silent colossus that rises three hundred and five feet, eleven inches above low water in our harbor and greets every ship that steams through the Narrows. . . .

Everything about the Statue of Liberty is enlightened, honest and noble. It has become everything it was intended to be. It is the Statue of "Liberty Enlightening the World," to use Bartholdi's original title for his heroic work. Out of good will and imagination some French people created a statue that has become one of the most precious of our natural resources.

Here is New York

From *Here Is New York,*
by E. B. White, copyright,
1949, by The Curtis Pub-
lishing Company, re-
printed by permission of
Harper & Brothers.

New York is the concentrate of art and commerce and sport and religion and entertainment and finance, bringing to a single compact arena the gladiator, the evangelist, the promoter, the actor, the trader and the merchant. It carries on its lapel the unexpungeable odor of the long past, so that no matter where you sit in New York you feel the vibrations of great times and tall deeds, of queer people and events and undertakings. . . .

There are roughly three New Yorks. There is, first, the New York of the man or woman who was born here, who takes the city for granted and accepts its size and its turbulence as natural and inevitable. Second, there is the New York of the commuter—the city that is devoured by locusts each day and spat out each night. Third, there is the New York of the person who was born some-where else and came to New York in quest of something. Of these three trembling cities the greatest is the last—the city of final destination, the city that is a goal. It is this third city that accounts for New York's high-strung disposition, its poetical deportment, its dedication to the arts, and its incom-parable achievements. Commuters give the city its tidal restlessness; natives give it solidity and continuity; but the settlers give it passion. And whether it is a farmer arriving from Italy to set up a small grocery store in a slum, or a young girl arriving from a small town in Mississippi to escape the indignity of being observed by her neighbors, or a boy arriving from the Corn Belt with a manuscript in his suitcase and a pain in his heart, it makes no difference: each embraces New York with the intense excitement of first love, each absorbs New York with the fresh eyes of an adventurer, each generates heat and light to dwarf the Consolidated Edison Company.

New York's Playground

From *New York Year By
Year,* by O. O. McIntyre,
a chapter in *America As
Americans See It,* edited
by Fred J. Ringel, copy-
right, 1932, by Harcourt,
Brace and Company, Inc.,
reprinted by permission.

Broadway is New York's playground, running slant-wise the entire length of the island called Manhattan. By day it is an ordinary street, rippling along with wholesale houses, chain drug stores, cafeterias, cinema temples, haber-dasheries, hotels, and dance halls. At night when its millions of electric lights burst into a blaze it is The Great White Way—the street that whips the uni-verse. It is both a high-ball and a head-ache, a delicately flanged bowl of champagne with roses floating on top and cruel thorns underneath—a paradox. There is a saying there is a broken heart for every light on Broadway. This may be only a lyrical sentimentality but certainly no street has lifted so many to fame and sent so many others hurtling to obscurity. They rise and fall quickly on Broadway and no one stops to glance at the clay feet.

The Lincoln Memorial

From *Washington Today,* copyright ©, 1955, by Eleanor Early, reprinted by permission of Prentice-Hall, Inc., Englewood Cliffs, N. J.

If most tourists could visit only one place in Washington, they probably would choose the Washington Monument. But I'd go to the Lincoln Memorial. And if I could recapture the thrill I got the first time, I wouldn't care if I never went anywhere else. Seeing the statue under perfect conditions is like visiting a cathedral when nobody is around. It is wonderful at any time. But when the crowds go away, it is like something in a dream. The first time I saw it was in the winter. The moon was shining; the air was still and beautiful. In the magic of the night, the temple became a holy place, and Lincoln seemed to be the saddest man in the world.

The building, designed by Henry Bacon, is of white marble, built like a Greek temple, with a pillared colonnade of thirty-six columns, representing the states of the Union at the time of Lincoln's death. Within the building are more columns, fifty feet high, which divide the interior into three chambers. In the middle one is the statue of Lincoln. . . . Lincoln sits in a marble armchair in the center of the open temple, and looks out upon the world. The chair is mounted on a high pedestal lighted from above, so that the face and body are illuminated in a striking manner. The statue, a completely realistic figure, is nineteen feet tall. Its solitary grandeur makes it appear larger, and Lincoln's sad eyes seem to look on all the sorrow of the earth.

From the Top of the Washington Monument

From *Washington Is Wonderful,* copyright ©, 1956, by Dorothea R. Jones, reprinted by permission of Harper & Brothers.

The view from the top, no matter how many times you may see it, is breathtaking and will revitalize your mental geography of the city. . . . As you peer out of the north windows, there is the White House in miniature, looking serenely beautiful, secure, and well cared for. By all means, look eastward and salute the Capitol, Washington's other skyline landmark, standing head and shoulders above the city. No unsightly canal splits the green Mall as it did one hundred years ago. Look east across to the red turrets of the Smithsonian Institution, called "Uncle Sam's Attic." Around to the southeast you'll see the Department of Agriculture's vast buildings, with not so much as a hint of the old stockyards located on that site during the Civil War. . . . Across from Agriculture, you'll look down on the Bureau of Engraving and Printing's sprawling operation.

Before you turn away, let your eyes move west of the White House, past the old State Department Building to Seventeenth Street, N.W. Follow the street south as it crosses Constitution Avenue—that's the broad, tree-lined thoroughfare which separates the Monument from the parklike Ellipse. The Zero Milestone, from which all distances on the continent are supposed to be computed, is located here, nine hundred feet south of the White House.

Mount Desert, Maine

From *Trending Into Maine,* copyright, 1938, by Kenneth Roberts and N. C. Wyeth, reprinted by permission of Doubleday & Company, Inc.

Mount Desert has a unique combination of mountain and sea that sets it apart from all other resorts. Unique, too, is Bar Harbor's strange combination of mountainous social elegances and shaggy simplicity, which leads summer visitors to build magnificent mansions in which to entertain admiring friends; then to build log cabins far off in the deep woods to which they sulkily retire to escape the social activities made necessary by their mansions.

From Champlain, who first gave the island its name, down to John Greenleaf Whittier, men have spoken as highly of the beauties of Mount Desert as it's possible to speak. "From the summit of Green Mountain," wrote an anonymous visitor in 1866, "the view is one of unparalleled wonder. Half ocean, half land, and the middle distance a bright mosaic of island and bay, it stretches from far Katahdin at the north, a hundred and twenty miles as the crow flies, to an unlimited distance over the sea." . . .

Boston: Relic and Type

From *About Boston,* copyright, 1948, by David McCord, reprinted by permission of the author and Little, Brown and Company.

A city never seems quite so young as it does in the spring, or quite so old as it does in the winter. At the turning point of the seasons Boston is at once both old and new; and perhaps she won't mind if we stop for a moment to look at her. Why should she mind? The country, and indeed the world, has looked at her with mingled admiration, affection, and alarm for something more than three centuries. Three centuries is a long time in the annals of America. It is time enough to build a city—time enough to marry bricks and mortar, cornice and cobblestone, roof tile and chimney pot; twisted streets and squares and avenues; fences, bridges, and trees; Common and parks; docks and markets and graveyards; color and flavor and vista; spires and the sprinkle of bells; time enough to contrive a city by the sea and give her true grace and noble definition. The blending of all these things material and immaterial was completed in an earlier century than ours, but the marvel of Boston is that the blend has somehow survived. Roundabout and even within the old town has grown the new; but the original profile is still there, like the fine Roman nose in a Copley portrait, and all the traffic and bewilderment of modern life have not changed it very much.

On the page opposite is a photograph of Stowe, Vermont. Stowe is the skier's delight and is one of the country's famous winter resorts.

Sugaring in New Hampshire

From *The Great White Hills of New Hampshire*, copyright, 1946, by Ernest Poole, reprinted by permission of Willis Kingsley Wing.

The long story of sugaring had been begun by Indian squaws, who drove into the maples small wooden taps, gathered the sap in bark cups hung beneath and poured it into huge bowls of wood and, by dropping in hot rocks from fires close by, heated the sap and so boiled it down to a thick syrup, blackened by the sooty stones. This they mixed with bear's grease and into the dark rich mixture they dipped roast venison and corn bread. Learning from them, our farmers at first sugared in the open. With sumac stems they tapped the trees, caught the sap in small buckets beneath, gathered it in big wooden pails carried on hand sleds or shoulder yokes and poured it into huge kettles hung on poles between forked posts, with a fire underneath. From such beginnings the work was developed to that of today, when the sap is gathered from tin buckets on trees into copper tanks set upon horse-drawn sleds and is hauled to the sugarhouse, built of frame or of logs, with a cupola on the roof to let out the clouds of steam from sap boiling in the evaporator below.

I shall never forget the fairy tinkle of sap into pails on our six hundred trees, the bounce and crash of the big tank sled moving slowly up and down slopes to the trough running into our sugarhouse, nor the water-like sap that steamed inside, first to white and then to golden foam, to be skimmed until it "flaked off" right and then to be drawn and strained into gallon cans of amber syrup. I remember a night when a big full moon poured its radiance through bare branches down upon the clean deep snow, and not a sound but the hoot of an owl and the low roar and crackle of the log fire in our house.

The Island of Nantucket

From *Moby Dick,* by Herman Melville.

Nantucket! Take out your map and look at it. See what a real corner of the world it occupies; how it stands there, away off shore, more lonely than the Eddystone lighthouse. Look at it—a mere hillock, and elbow of sand; all beach, without a background. There is more sand than you would use in twenty years as a substitute for blotting paper. Some gamesome wights will tell you that they have to plant weeds there, they don't grow naturally; that they import Canada thistles; that they have to send beyond seas for a spile to stop a leak in an oil cask; that pieces of wood in Nantucket are carried about like bits of the true cross in Rome; that people there plant toadstools before their houses, to get under the shade in summer time; that one blade of grass makes an oasis, three blades in a day's walk a prairie; that they wear quicksand shoes, something like Laplander snowshoes; that they are so shut up, belted about, every way inclosed, surrounded, and made an utter island of by the ocean, that to their very chairs and tables small clams will sometimes be found adhering, as to the backs of sea turtles. But these extravaganzas only show that Nantucket is no Illinois.

Niagara Falls

From *North America,* by Anthony Trollope.

Of all the sights of this earth of ours which tourists travel to see—at least of all those which I have seen—I am inclined to give the palm to the Falls of Niagara. In the catalogue of such sights I intend to include all buildings, pictures, statues, and wonders of art made by man's hands, and also all beauties of nature prepared by the Creator for the delight of his creatures. This is a long word; but as far as my taste and judgment go, it is justified. I know no other one thing so beautiful, so glorious, and so powerful. I would not by this be understood as saying that a traveler wishing to do the best with his time should first of all seek Niagara. . . . At Niagara there is the fall of waters alone. But that fall is more graceful than Giotto's tower, more noble than the Apollo. The peaks of the Alps are not more astounding in their solitude. The valleys of the Blue Mountains in Jamaica are less green. The finished glaze of life in Paris is less invariable; and the full tide of trade around the Bank of England is not so inexorably powerful.

Newport, 1870

From *The Sentimental Tourist—Early American Travels, 1870–1871,* by Henry James, reprinted by permission of Paul R. Reynolds & Son, New York.

The place consists, as the reader will know, of an ancient and honorable town, a goodly harbor, and a long, broad neck of land, stretching southward into the sea and forming the chief habitation of the summer colony. Along the greater part of its eastward length, this projecting coast is bordered with cliffs of no great height, and dotted with seaward-gazing villas. At the head of the promontory the villas enjoy a magnificent reach of prospect. The pure Atlantic—the old world westward tides—expire directly at their feet. Behind the line of villas runs the Avenue, with more villas yet—of which there is nothing at all to say but that those built recently are a hundred times prettier than those built fifteen years ago, and give one some hope of a revival of the architectural art. Some years ago, when I first knew Newport, the town proper was considered remarkably quaint. If an antique shabbiness that amounts almost to squalor is a pertinent element, as I believe it is, of this celebrated quality, the little main street at least—Thames Street by name—still deserves the praise. Here, in their crooked and dwarfish wooden mansions, are the shops that minister to the daily needs of the expanded city; and here of a summer morning, jolting over the cobble stones of the narrow roadway, you may see a hundred superfine ladies seeking with languid eagerness what they may buy —to "buy something," I believe, being a diurnal necessity of the conscientious American woman. This busy region gradually melts away into the grass-grown stillness of the Point, in the eyes of many persons the pleasantest quarter of Newport. . . .

May at Monticello

From *North With the Spring,* copyright ©, 1951, by Edwin Way Teale, reprinted by permission of Dodd, Mead & Company.

On that May morning one hundred twenty springs had passed since Jefferson died on his mountaintop overlooking the valley where he was born. One hundred sixty years had gone by since he published his *Notes on Virginia.* Yet the natural history of Monticello remained virtually unchanged. Bluebirds sang on the fence posts. Phoebes flitted in and out of the open doors of the old stables. A robin had built its nest at the top of one of the white columns of the west portico. And brown thrashers ran across the grass beneath an ancient linden tree that once provided shade for the third President of the United States.

Off to the east, beyond the mountainside where spring-clad trees stretched in a tumbling sea down the slope toward the Piedmont, a trio of turkey buzzards swung slowly, curving on the wind, hanging on the updrafts, drifting far out over the sides, then sliding back to go riding low above Monticello.

The birds of Monticello provide one of the outstanding memories of a naturalist's visit. The trees provide another. Here, rooted where Thomas Jefferson had planted them in the eighteenth century, stood ancient tulips, lindens, copper beeches, sugar maples, European larches. Here were noble trees, patriarchs that brought to mind Sir Thomas Browne's observation of long ago: "Generations pass while some trees stand and old families last not three oaks."

Yellowstone Park

From *Sweet Land,* copyright, 1934, by Lewis Gannett, reprinted by permission of Doubleday & Company, Inc.

Yellowstone, first of the national parks, was made such because of its spurting geysers, its steaming hot springs, its glass mountain, its painted canyon. . . .

Geysers are startling, weird, spectacular; the colors of the boiling springs are marvelous; the gay yellows and reds of the strange soft-rocked canyon are exciting; but Yellowstone excited us most of all as a lovely bit of mountain wilderness, where elk and moose and beaver, bison and antelope and mountain sheep, seemed to live as they had lived in pre-Columbian days, yet strangely unafraid of man. Here again, as a hundred times before, we yearned for time to make pack trips back from the automobile road; but here the automobile roads were themselves incredibly fresh and beautiful. The thick forests of that persistent lodgepole pine, which seeds itself so thickly after every fire that sometimes the forests, almost too thick for human penetration, are made up of five- or six-inch trunks that waver skyward for a hundred feet; the high willowed meadows where the moose hid; the lovely alpine gardens toward the top of Mount Washburn, where the mountain sheep browsed and the lupine stretched in great blue beds straight from the edge of July snowdrifts, and the white phlox echoed the snow's color lower down; the twinflower that hid beneath a waterfall; the pale yellow columbine and deep golden asters; the weird elephant's-head flowers by the roadsides. . . .

San Francisco

From *Don't Call It Frisco,* copyright, 1953, by Herb Caen, reprinted by permission of Doubleday & Company, Inc.

The tourist, looking at the city for the first time, shakes his head in a puzzled way and sighs: "This San Francisco—it sort of gets you. There's something about it. I don't know quite what it is, but it's something." . . .

And the San Franciscan smiles and nods, for he thinks he knows what it is. . . . It's the gay fluttering of the flags and pennants on the downtown minarets, outlined against a blue sky flecked with fast-rolling fog. . . . It's the never-cloying thrill of standing at the bow of a proud old ferryboat as it churns its white way in an arc across the Bay and then eased, like a practiced firehorse, into its slip under the Ferry Building's ageless tower. . . . It's the pride, reborn again and again, that comes when you stand on a Marin mountain-top and gaze over the water at your magic city, gleaming like an endless mosaic that covers each hill with castles and fills each valley with romantic lights and shadows. . . . It's the metropolitan stage setting that unfolds before your eyes from Twin Peaks—the solid, stolid Mission, where each house is a time-touched landmark; Market Street cutting its steamroller swath across a field of concrete and leaving a trail of neon; and, in the far distance, the Bay Bridge hunching its thin shoulders and reaching out to clutch the Oakland shore with fingers of steel.

Chinese New Year in San Francisco

From *Bay Window Bohemia,* copyright © 1956, by Oscar Lewis, reprinted by permission of Doubleday & Company, Inc.

By far the most colorful—and noisy—of city-wide holidays was Tong Yan Sun Neen, known to the Occidental heathen as Chinese New Year, which annually took place in late January or early February. Then for a period of seven days a carnival spirit held sway throughout Chinatown, during which its entire population, augmented by thousands of countrymen from far and near, jammed its narrow steets and alleys while the whole central part of the city echoed day and night with a continuous roar.

The source of the noise was of course firecrackers, prodigious numbers of which were set off during the week-long celebrations, their avowed purpose being to scare off any evil spirits that might be hovering about bent on spoiling the fun. It was a period of rejoicing and good will, when bills were paid, gifts exchanged, and the residents, decked out in their most festive costumes, exchanged ceremonious calls. Some of the outfits—those of prosperous merchants and their women and progeny—were extraordinarily colorful: rich silks resplendent with embroideries and gold ornaments set off with jade and semiprecious stones.

The high point of the week came on the final day, when the Lion—a resplendent dragon symbolizing good luck—was paraded through the streets, its head pausing at each doorway to receive gifts set out for it, and its long, undulating body, supported by scores of celebrants, trailing along behind.

171

Oak Alley Plantation

From *Plantation Parade: The Grand Manner in Louisiana,* copyright, 1945, by Harnett T. Kane, reprinted by permission of William Morrow and Company.

Oak Alley (today) shines in a beauty with which the original could probably not compare. To the work of man, nature has added its hand. The oaks are in full splendor; any one of them would rank as a giant, and all twenty-eight remain. The master growth among them has a circumference of twenty-one feet at its "waist"; the rest are not noticeably less imposing. Though the trunks rise almost ninety feet apart across the open lawn, their upper branches overlap, meeting in the air to create an arch of gnarled brown, the thick foliage twining and intertwining. . . . The nameless planter could hardly have pictured a final result such as this; nothing that he had known in Europe could have prepared him for the reality that was to come.

At the height of the day's sunlight, long streaks of yellow fall through the openings in the oaks to the grass below. At most other times the approach is a twilight one, tree after tree forming a canopy of magnificently symmetrical arrangement. The lower branches end at the same height down the line; the effect is almost that of a stage setting, though more enormous than man could achieve. To the back sits the house, framed by its trees on each side of the aisle. . . . The trees, running perpendicularly to the river, shield the house until the passerby is directly before it; and there it stands forth, complete.

The King Ranch in Texas

From *Texas: A World in Itself,* copyright, 1942, by George Sessions Perry, reprinted by permission of the author's Estate.

In many ways the King Ranch is unique, yet it is probably Texas' most representative institution. Like Texas, it is the biggest of its kind, almost violently progressive, marked by some dissention, full of vinegar, and making money. The "little pasture" of the King Ranch is 6,000 acres. Three others are 65,000 acres each. Though the Klebergs (a Kleberg married Captain King's daughter) are horse-riding, gun-toting, genuine ranch folk, the ranch has been mechanized and organized to the hilt. Lesser methods could hardly keep its gigantic processes in flux. For example, a spring shipment of 17,000 head (shipping charges: $100,000) could not be profitably shipped to market without the most careful timing and efficiency, since every delay means a loss in weight of valuable beef. For one thing, the King loaders use electric prods for quickening the pace of sluggard animals in the loading pens and chutes. . . . The King Ranch incorporates most of the kinds of land to be found in the state, from coastal marsh to desert, which gives it a good jockeying position in its conflict with the elements. When drouth strikes its inland domains, there will be grass of a kind on its coastal ranges. Surrounding its various pastures there are 1,500 miles of fence. Its cow hands, unlike those in the Panhandle who are Anglo-Saxon and those around Beaumont who are chiefly French boys and Negroes, are Mexican *vaqueros.*

Dinosaur National Monument

From *This Is Dinosaur:* Echo Park Country and Its Magic Rivers, Edited by Wallace Stegner, copyright, 1955, by Alfred A. Knopf, Inc., reprinted by permission.

Dinosaur National Monument is one of the last almost "unspoiled" wildnernesses—which means it is relatively unmarked by man. . . . What shall we say of it? That it is a three-pronged district of about 200,000 acres, straddling the Utah-Colorado border a little south of where that border meets the southern boundary of Wyoming. That it is a part—one of the junior partners—of the National Park System begun with the reservation of Yellowstone in 1872 and confirmed by the establishment of the National Park Service in 1916. That topographically it is defined by the deep canyons of two rivers, the Green and the Yampa, which meet secretly in the sunny, sunken pocket of Echo Park and then cut Whirlpool Canyon, Island Park, Rainbow Park, and Split Mountain Canyon, from whose mouth the water breaks out into the open Uinta Valley of Utah. That the plateau through which the canyons are cut is an eastward extension of the Uinta Mountains, one of the few east-west-trending ranges in the United States. That the larger of the two rivers, the Green, is the longest fork of the Colorado; and that it used to be called the Seedskeedee-Agie, the Prairie Hen River, by the Crows, and by the Spaniards the Rio Verde. Its tributary the Yampa is even yet by some people and some maps called the Bear.

One can observe that Echo Park, at the heart of this reserve, lies at approximately 109 West Longitude and 40.31 North Latitude; that the altitude ranges from 4700 feet at the mouth of Split Mountain Canyon to 9600 feet at the tip of Zenobia Peak near the northeastern boundary; that the rocks exposed run in age from the Uinta Mountains quartzite of the Pre-Cambrian period to the Brown's Park sandstone of the Pliocene; that the life zones represented spread from the Sonoran in the canyon bottoms to sub-arctic on the higher ridges. The colors of the rocks vary from a rich red-brown to vermilion, from gray to almost sugar-white, with many shades of pink and buff and salmon in between. The cliffs and sculptured forms are sometimes smooth, sometimes fantastically craggy, always massive, and they have a peculiar capacity to excite the imagination; the effect on the human spirit is neither numbing nor awesome, but warm and infinitely peaceful.

On the following double-page spread is a photograph of St. Lucia, the Windward Islands. St. Lucia offers tourists a balmy climate and many fine hotels.

173

Harbor of Charlotte Amalie

From *The Complete Handbook of the Virgin Islands,* by Stuart Murray, copyright, 1951, by Duell, Sloan & Pearce, Inc., reprinted by permission.

Today, in this harbor of Charlotte Amalie, once frequented by the colorful and daring pirates of history, the old and picturesque waterfront is always busy with the comings and goings of the trim little schooners which ply between St. Thomas, St. John, St. Croix and the British Virgin Island, Tortola. Fishnets and sails flap loosely as they hang from tall masts to dry in the gentle breezes which sweep the harbor at all times. The docks swarm with activity as cargoes are unloaded and taken to warehouses or markets. St. Thomas imports meat, fish, and vegetables from Tortola and the weekly races of the Tortolamen sailing into the harbor in fleet formation is a sight that visitors seldom forget.

The hills of St. Thomas sweep rapidly upward from the colorful waterfront and appropriately reach their maximum altitude on the peak of Crown Mountain, high above the beaches and coves which string like beads around the shores. Massive, turbulent rock formations of ancient volcanic origin make up the twenty-eight square miles of St. Thomas' hills and dales and fascinating shorelines. From the heights one can see far into the bluegreen east across the peaks of St. John and Tortola and into the infinity that becomes the Leeward Islands in the curving necklace known as the Antilles chain.

The Prado, Heart of Havana

From *Havana, the Portrait of a City,* copyright, 1953, by W. Adolphe Roberts, reprinted by permission of Coward-McCann, Inc.

Most visitors in the old days saw Havana for the first time from the deck of a ship, with the Morro on the one side and the Punta on the other. Now the great majority come by plane and land at the Rancho Boyeros airport seventeen miles from the city. But whether they choose some outlying hotel or one in the center they soon realize that the Prado is the heart of things. It is the place from which to start out to note the sights, the restaurants, and the shops . . . the most delightful of streets at any time of day. From the waterfront to the Parque Central its raised promenade of mottled, reddish marble is shadowed by a thick canopy of laurels. The sidewalks on the far sides of the two driveways are in part under arcades, and at every few steps you find novelty shops, refreshment places, theaters, clubs, and travel offices. This is the lower Prado. The Parque Central, of no great size, is flanked by imposing structures such as the Centro Gallego and the Centro Asturiana, which are the homes of mutual aid societies, and the Manzana de Gomez, a combined office building and shopping mart.

Dally in the lower Prado. There are marble benches with high backs and broad armrests on its promenade, which the sanitary department sluices with water at sunrise until they gleam. The sea looks wonderfully blue at the end of the tunnel formed by the laurels.

Rafting Down the Rio Grande in Jamaica

From *Escape to the West Indies,* copyright, 1956, by Bradley Smith, reprinted by permission of Alfred A. Knopf, Inc.

Arrangements can be made in Port Antonio for Jamaica's most exciting scenic trip, rafting down the Rio Grande. . . . The first view of the raft is unprepossessing. A group of flat bamboo poles lashed together with wire and a seat built across the back third make up the vessel. A brawny, black, gleaming athlete with a long rafting pole completes the picture. As visitors arrive at the rafting center, the raftsmen argue over which boatload will go out first. . . .

The ideal costume for rafting is a bathing suit (so that you can go along for a swim along the way) plus a long-sleeved cotton shirt to shield you from too much sun. It is a good plan to take a thermos of rum, brandy, or lemonade, and a packet of sandwiches. Although the trip lasts only a little over one hour, a picnic along the way can be very pleasant. . . . Long vistas are revealed as the river winds its way down through quiet fields. As the buoyant craft descends, the river becomes narrower. Yellow and orange bamboo groves grow high along the banks. The tamarind tree and coconut palm crowd close along the shores. . . . Then comes the exhilaration of shooting the rapids. Although by no means dangerous, it is very exciting. The little craft turns and whirls as the raftsman guides it between rocks through the channel. Spray jets back through the bamboo frame. Shortly after the rapids, the end of the trip is reached. A short walk up the bank to the waiting car, and the exciting experience of rafting down the Rio Grande is over.

Port-au-Prince

From *Red, Black, Blonde and Olive,* copyright ©, Edmund Wilson, 1956, reprinted by permission of The Oxford University Press, Inc.

Port-au-Prince, the capital of Haiti, follows the curve of a lovely little harbor that may recall southern Italy, but only to lead you to note certain essential differences. The landscape of Italy is always solid, the color is likely to be laid on thick; but Port-au-Prince is insubstantial, with no sharp brightness or sudden contrasts.

Looking out from my second-floor verandah, over the railing of white wooden lace, I see below, in mid-afternoon, the shadowed green tree-tops and roofs of the loose-knit tropical town, and—beyond the rare sprinkling of spires and domes, the low bulks of public buildings, picked out, amid greenery, vivid white, and the warm red-and-blue of the Haitian flag that is flying from a wireless spindle—there stretches the blue of the water, varying as if with the shades of a sheet of *taffetas changeant,* pulled taut to the south in greenish shallows, to the north in a surface of a blue so tender that, though floating a white sail or two, it seems nothing so dense as saltwater but some element sheerly aesthetic, the discovery of a delicate water-colorist. Strips of cloud, not too heavily charged with rain, hang low over the bare coastal hills, which, though not far away, suggest mysteries.

Flying to Nassau

From *And So to America,* copyright, 1947, by Cecil Roberts, reprinted by permission of the author.

I found myself flying across a morning sea to Nassau. And what a sea! The shallows of this water, with hundreds of little atolls awash or barely submerged, offer every color of the rainbow, particularly to the aerial traveler who looks down into this submarine world. Past Cat Key and Bimini Islands he goes over a sea now translucently turquoise, now jade green, purple, aquamarine, mauve, lemon yellow and apricot rose. I have heard it described as the most colorful two-hour flight in the world and possibly it is so. I can imagine nothing more enchanting. One seems, a celestial voyager, to be looking down on a faery domain where the rainbow ends. Lonely little wisps of cloud sail past one like cherubs strayed out of the divine nursery whose ocean floor shimmers with its kaleidoscopic carpet. And then comes that curving descent to Prince's Island, Nassau, shining white amid its jungle-green vegetation.

My hosts dwelt across the harbor, on Hog Island, in an enchanting South Sea house of rushes, bamboo, lattice work and a cockatoo-haunted patio. It is an ugly name for a strip of sand that is more rightly called, at its extremity, Paradise Beach. Immediately below our verandah was a sandy shore. A few steps and we were bathing in water of such blueness and warmth as only tropical islands know. We dined by day in the bird-haunted patio to a trilling of canaries, and sometimes as we sat at cocktails the quick green lizards scuttled in and out of the rockery. Perhaps evening was the most enchanting of all with the moon upon the water, and the blinking of the lighthouse, the soft warm air of those perfect January nights.

Hamilton Harbor, Bermuda

From *Bermuda Journey,* copyright, 1946, by William E. S. Zuill, reprinted by permission of Coward-McCann, Inc.

The most interesting thing about Hamilton is, of course, the water front and harbor with the ever-changing panorama unfolding like a perpetual movie reel. Ferryboats come and go; rowboats lazily ply across to Paget; old sailboats with rusty sails beat slowly up the harbor with freight for the western parishes; fishing craft come alongside the wharf to sell their catch; speedboats dash hither and yon with proud disdain for smaller and slower craft; a steam tug from the Dockyard arrives with naval personnel and womenfolk for a day in town; a tender full of passengers from a cruise ship is welcomed by carriage drivers and townspeople; freighters from America, from England, and from the Argentine tie up at the lower docks; a schooner with lumber from Florida berths near the center of the town; liners from New York and from Canada appear regularly with passengers and freight—such are the activities of this small but busy port.

Mexico City

Mexico City, with a population approaching four million, is the heart of a country that is more Indian than European, more European than North American, yet so Americanized that steel-girdered skyscrapers now rise steadily from the marshy lake bed of the ancient Aztec capital. It is a city of bustle and great wealth, a city of parks and flowers, a city of teeming business where the lavish Continental Hilton lifts its curved height from the Paseo de la Reforma, one among many luxurious hostelries catering to the tourist from the north, with a service that is modern and decorations that are steeped in the colorful Indian past of Mexico.

Mexico is color and contrast. Even in the cool capital, 7,486 feet above the sea, are all the colors of tropical birds—in the great murals, in the stone mosaics at University City, in the bright tones of the fabulous homes in the Gardens of the Pedregal. And a stone's throw from all this modernity and all this wealth, beggars living in shacks on vacant lots, urchins in rags, poverty that is hopeless, diseased, and overwhelming. . . . Mexico is made up of such contrasts, and in the capital these contrasts may be seen on a vast scale.

Guadalajara

Every morning of our week's stay in Guadalajara we awakened to the whisk of the street cleaner's broom and began our daily wanderings through the city. Sometimes we rode a horse-drawn carriage while the clipperty-clop of the hoofs rang through quiet streets. We caught glimpses of radiant gardens behind sterile walls or watched children leave for school, blue and white uniforms neat and books like knapsacks on their backs. Or sometimes we walked to the central market, where the commercial heart of the people beat its unchanging rhythm under the steel ribs of a block-square concrete building. With the crowd we pushed between shaded stalls outside, past the saddles and bolts of bright cloth, the sandals made from tires and the tinsmith hammering ladles from old cans. We watched a boy scrape the insulation from wire and a girl weave the wire into a basket. Nothing was wasted except time. On the corner a street magician chanted his patter to an indifferent audience while nearby an old woman shrouded in her shawl slept by the wares no one bought, her gentle snores accompaniment to the unceasing pat-pat of hands making tortillas. Through the iron gates of the market poured an overwhelming dissonance of smells. Meat, covered with flies, hung in strips, thick wheels of yellow cheese overpowered the fragrance of adjoining flower stands, and next to them vegetables formed high pyramids on the floor. Stems of bananas swayed in one corner and one giant variety was new to me. I asked its name and smiled at the answer. Another reminder of Mexico's emphasis on man.

179

Ceremonial Costumes of Guatemala

From *Four Keys to Guatemala,* by Vera Kelsey and Lilly de Jongh Osborne, copyright, 1939, 1943, 1946, 1948, 1952, by Vera Kelsey, reprinted by permission of Funk & Wagnalls Company.

Considering the fate of the indigenous costume in other parts of the world, that the dress of the Indians of Guatemala has survived with only relatively minor changes is further testimony to its tribal significance. Even now, whatever they may wear on ordinary days, Indians of mountain and highland villages retain intact the ceremonial costume for social or religious occasions. . . . The richness of an Indian costume is in the textiles and embroideries, not in the style. Except for the trousers worn by the men of some tribes, each garment is practically made when it leaves the loom. A hole is cut in a straight length for the head, a few stitches taken at the sides to make a woman's blouse. Skirts are wrapped tightly around the hips or laid in pleats about the waist. Another blouse made on the same lines, thrown over the shoulders when the air chills, serves as cloak or cape. Everything else is a straight or square piece folded or tied to fit.

Lake Nicaragua

From *The World's Great Lakes,* copyright, 1948, by Ferdinand C. Lane, reprinted by permission of the author.

Nicaragua lies in the republic of that name, its western shore but sixteen miles from the Pacific, its eastern somewhat more distant from the Atlantic. One hundred and ten miles long and 45 in width, its area is 3089. Once it was even more extensive, uniting with Lake Managua, 38 miles by 16, which also fills part of the valley. This valley, a former gulf of the Pacific, was dammed off by volcanic upheaval and its imprisoned waters changed from salt to fresh. Managua, higher by fifteen feet, now drains into Nicaragua through the Tipitapa River, an eccentric stream whose frequent stretches of dry bed overlie subterranean channels.

Both lakes are the handiwork of the volcanoes. Grim cones not only frown from the hinterland but encroach upon the shore line and emerge as islands from the lake floor. Several are still smoldering, led by fire-breathing Momotombo. Two volcanoes, Concepcion and Madera, have coalesced to form Ometepe Island, 20 miles long, which lies halfway up Lake Nicaragua's western shore. Concepcion erupted in 1883 and has shown signs of more recent truculence. Near this island the lake reaches its greatest depth, about 200 feet. Smaller islets are so beautiful in the morning light that the natives call them "diamonds."

Nicaragua reveals its oceanic origin in such marine life as sharks, sawfish, and that giant of the herring family, the tarpon. Sharks, acclimated to its fresh waters, have evolved a unique species, *Eulamia nicaraguensis,* found nowhere else. These unwelcome intruders, which may weigh two hundred pounds or more, are true man-eaters, for scarcely a season passes that some swimmer does not fall victim to their voracity. Two species of sawfish also occur, one producing specimens weighing over seven hundred pounds.

The Famous Golden Altar of San José

From *Panama of Today,* by A. Hyatt Verrill, copyright ©, 1927, by Dodd, Mead and Company, Inc., reprinted by permission.

Beyond Santo Domingo and its arch . . . is a church—an obscure, unattractive, severely plain structure which might well be passed unnoticed, but which is probably the most noteworthy sight in Panama City, for within its portals is the famous golden altar of San José. Marvelously beautiful is the effect of this magnificent altar of gold as the sunlight, streaming through the stained glass windows gleams upon its burnished surface and is reflected in dazzling brilliancy. And fascinating and interesting as the altar itself is the romantic story of its history. Of beaten gold, and worth a king's ransom, the altar, so legend says, was the pride of the richest church in Old Panama—then the richest and most important city in the New World—and was made from the church's tithe of the gold from Panama's mines and the looted treasure of Peru.

Many romantic tales of this altar have been told. One has it that the famous altar was taken down and carried to sea when word of Morgan's coming reached Old Panama. . . . But the true story as related by one of the priests of San José church, and which is borne out by documentary evidence, is scarcely less romantic and is just as interesting. According to this the altar was disguised when the famous buccaneer marched across the Isthmus to Old Panama. But instead of being taken down and hurried by ship to safety on the high seas, the altar remained in the doomed city and was saved owing to the fact that San José church was the one church that escaped the conflagration which swept the town. Thus preserved as if by a miracle, the altar was later removed to the new church in the present Panama where it still remains.

On the following double-page spread is Rio de Janeiro's trade-mark, Sugar Loaf Mountain—1,296 feet high, which guards the entrance to Guanabara Bay.

181

Arrival at Rio

From *Rio,* by Hugh Gibson, copyright, 1937, by Doubleday & Company, Inc., reprinted by permission.

The haze lifted and a scene met our eyes which made all the written descriptions seem trivial and absurd. It was so much more wonderful than our bravest imaginings. One thing we learned then and there—that the bay and its setting cannot be described though many of the world's best writers have had a fling at it. If you want to know what Rio is like you cannot learn it from a book. There is only one way—come and see for yourself. The best a book can do for you is to give you the bare bones which may help you to get your bearings. To the right, as we come in, the fort of Santa Cruz guards the entrance to the harbor—ancient cannon showing their muzzles through the thick walls and the seas surging angrily against the sloping rocks on which the fort is built. On the other side of the entrance stands the fort of Sao Joao—less than a mile separates them—and dead ahead, due north, forming the top of a triangle, is the low-lying Lage Fort—the only modern one of the three. Still farther ahead the low island of Villegaignon, from which rises the gray bulk of the Naval Academy. . . . Farther to the left, the Sugar Loaf, the giant sentinel, the Dois Irmaos (Two Brothers), and farther away the sail-like form of Gavea, half hiding the fading line of mountains which stretches away down the coast to Rio Grande do Sul. From Santa Cruz there is another range of mountains raising its picturesque headlands away to Cabo Frio on the one hand and on the other to the Organ Mountains, which form a blue backdrop beyond the bay. Towering above the town is the summit of the Corcovado, with its statue of the Redeemer.

Brazil's Old King Coffee

From *America Faces South,* by T. R. Ybarra, copyright ©, 1939, by Dodd, Mead and Company, Inc., reprinted by permission.

If you would see Old King Coffee in all his glory, go to southern Brazil, into the land of the renowned "red earth," where coffee shrubs blossom sometimes for a full hundred years; where they spread themselves before you in countless thousands until they vanish over the edge of the horizon, flanked by banana trees, their faithful henchmen, and guarded by palm trees, their slender sentinels. Enjoy the hospitality of a *fazenda*—as they call a plantation in Brazil—where you will find modernity going hand in hand with an old-fashioned welcome to casual visitors which is like a fragrant breeze from a past of leisure and courtliness. Yes, go to the land of the "red earth"—and I guarantee you will never again look upon your morning cup of coffee as something to be gulped down indifferently, with one eye on the paper and the other on your watch, lest you arrive late downtown. Never again!

Old King Coffee's realm is centered in the Brazilian state of São Paulo, and the place where he holds court is the city of São Paulo, southern Brazil's metropolis, and the port whence he sends out yearly billions of coffee berries for brewing the world's favorite beverage is Santos. . . .

The Pavements of Rio

The Cariocas have done so many things to add to the natural beauty of their city that it is difficult to determine which one should be mentioned first. But the famous pavements are doubtless the most distinctive. . . . When one stops to think that nothing strikes the eye so persistently as the pavement it does seem strange that there have been such few and futile attempts to relieve it of its drab ugliness. Even in parks in other cities they are ugly. That is the reason the highly decorated pavements of Rio strike one so forcibly and appear so unreal. . . . Instead of an expanse of unattractive cement the pavement is composed of intricate patterns made of irregularly shaped blocks of black and white marble. It is the biggest mosaic in the world for it embraces in its decorative scheme an entire city of a million and a half population.

The designs are of infinite variety. There are dozens of different borders, fleur de lis, circles, elaborate floral attempts, triangles, squares—in fact every conventional design I can think of except the swastika. The most common design is suggestive of the conventional wave to be seen in old Chinese sculpture and more modern Japanese prints. Thus the very pavements suggest a continuation of the waves which pound ceaselessly on the miles of gleaming sandy beach.

The Buenos Aires Café

Visitors just down from the United States sometimes feel that since Argentines spend so much time in their cafés they can't get much business done. *Portenos* disagree. They that feel the café is an essential part of their normal routine. As one man put it: "We accomplish as much over a café table as you do in your office. And it's far more convenient. A telephone call costs only twenty *centavos,* though it used to be free. Besides, there is no eavesdropping secretary to listen in. One's friends are here with the inside story of the Finance Ministry's latest move—or the newest scandal. Besides, *señor,* in what office can one get all of this service, plus food, and those lovely *señoritas* passing just outside the window all at the same time?" Whatever happens in Buenos Aires —and to a relative degree in the interior—is pretty thoroughly worked out in the cafés beforehand. The Argentine café has a social and political significance hard for an outsider to visualize. It may be a smart place in town, a neighborhood café which spreads out to the sidewalk, or a remote provincial *boliche.* All have a collection of tiny, marble-topped tables, back-breaking chairs, and a long service bar presided over by a portly, chit-dispensing proprietor at the elaborate, imported National Cash Register.

Inca Ruins of Machu Picchu, Peru

From *Highway of the Sun,* copyright ©, 1955, by Victor W. von Hagen, reprinted by permission of Duell, Sloan and Pearce.

The ruins of Machu Picchu—no one knows its original name—lie in a topographical saddle between the peaks of Machu (old) and Huayna Picchu (new). In this saddle is a complex of terraces, gabled stone houses, temples, sacred plazas and residence compounds, and the famous Inti-huatana sundials. In its magnificent position, Machu Picchu is the climax of a series of terraced cities along the Urubamba Gorge. Essentially a fortified city, its strongly constructed houses were most probably defense units. There was but one gate into the city, which, like most *pucaras,* was a self-sustaining unit whose terraces, following the contours of the mountains like a gigantic flight of steps, were planted to sustain its people. There were buildings of polished and well-fitted granite ashlars presumably designed for chieftains, a large place for the Sun Virgins, cruder clan-houses for the common people, barracks for soldiers, and even a prison. All the buildings had once been thatched with straw while the interiors were Spartan in their severity. The Indian slept on the ground on a woolen poncho; and with the usual tapestry hung over the door to keep out the night breezes, the three-legged pots placed over the fire for cooking, a brazier for warming the house, and a few decorations, the house of one who lived in Machu Picchu was complete. . . .

Fabled Lake Titicaca

From *The World's Great Lakes,* copyright, 1948, by Ferdinand C. Lane, reprinted by permission of the author.

Loftiest of the world's big lakes is Titicaca. Its wind-tormented surface, 12,507 feet above the neighboring Pacific, fills the deeper recesses of an interior basin thrust skyward for nearly two and a half miles by vast upheavals, and barred from the outside world by the still loftier Andes. . . . Titicaca forms part of the boundary between Bolivia and Peru. One hundred and twenty-five miles long with an extreme width of 41, it covers approximately 3200 square miles. Along the eastern shore a deep trough shows soundings of 892 feet. On the whole, however, the lake averages little more than a hundred, and steamers sometimes run aground on submerged mudbanks.

The coast line, in places, is abrupt, in others gently sloping. Along the western shore the scarp is concealed by vast lava flows from distant volcanoes, long dormant or extinct, which notch the sky line at heights of twenty thousand feet or more. Elsewhere the shores are low and swampy, lush with rank vegetation, where giant tortora reeds or bulrushes higher than a man's head provide not only fodder for cattle but materials for baskets, mats, and roofing thatch. Still stranger is their use in the picturesque reed boats or blasas, which have navigated Titicaca from immemorial times. Propelled by sails of finer reeds, these odd craft, which commonly last about two years, must be dried out occasionally to avoid becoming waterlogged.

La Paz

From *From Sea to Sea in South America,* copyright, 1953, by W. T. Blake, reprinted by permission of The McBride Company.

La Paz is an extraordinary city in many ways. It is the highest capital in the world, lying 12,400 feet above sea level, surrounded by mountains which run up nearly another 2000 feet to the Alto Plano, or High Plateau of the Andes, of which the western part of Bolivia is composed. The climate is cool in summer and cold in winter and the air so rarefied that visitors find difficulty in moving about and even sleeping during the first few days. . . .

The Indians are usually short in stature, broad and well built, with somewhat flat faces, and flattish noses, high cheekbones, very dark brown or black eyes and straight black hair. Their skin ranges in color between olive and light brown. Their dress is a matter of considerable interest, particularly in the case of women. . . . The women . . . are colorfully dressed and have a distinct costume of their own. Being a man I find it somewhat difficult to describe their garments, but it appears to me that the top part consists of a cotton or coarse linen blouse or chemise, which disappears into a very voluminous petticoat, over which are worn several more skirts, giving the women an extremely bulky appearance. At Carnival time and on Feast Days these skirts are of lovely and always bright materials, sometimes of velvet, sometimes of beautifully worked brocades and sometimes of plush.

Caracas — A City of Dreams

From *Crossroads of the Carribean Sea,* by Hendrik de Leeuw, copyright, December, 1935, by Julian Messner, Inc., reprinted by permission of the author.

Caracas lies three thousand feet above sea level in the fertile and lovely valley of Aragon, where it was founded by the Spanish adventurer and conqueror of Venezuela, Diego Lozado. . . . Caracas is a city of contrasts, where high-powered motorcars roll through a traffic glutted with pack mules, with cargadores staggering under heavy burdens, flower carriers, Martinique cooks carrying huge baskets of fruit on their heads, mounted caballeros. . . . Women gowned in Paris frocks ride in luxurious limousines over smooth boulevards, and bobbed-haired girls trip unaccompanied down narrow sidewalks. . . .

Block after block in sombre monotony rise the houses, Spanish in type, with red tiled roofs. Mantilla-wrapped women pass in and out, through the patios. High over the residences point the church spires. There are beautiful parks and palm-shaded squares and ancient doorways whose spike-studded gates have answered the call and knocking of the last three centuries. . . . We found its doors ever open to entertain us, with a warmth of welcome unmatched in all our travels. Lapped in the gentle balm of everlasting spring, embraced by slopes covered with coffee fincas and mountains that lift themselves thousands of feet above her glistening domes and spires, Caracas is magically beautiful, lovely as a city of dreams.

Colombians

From *Colombia, Gateway to South America,* copyright, 1941, by Kathleen Romoli, reprinted by permission of Doubleday & Company, Inc.

When someone turns around between Martinis and asks brightly, "Tell me, what are the Colombians like?" he creates a mild problem. Should one be adequate and take a chance on holding the listener's attention to one subject a quarter of an hour—always a reckless gamble—or just pare truth to the bone and answer "Charming"? . . .

In the widest sense of the word, a Colombian may be any one of several extremes. He may be tall and blond and blue eyed, or small and brown and Asiatic looking. Or he may be black. He may wear the clothes of Savile Row and boots by Yapp, or he may be shod in *alpargatas,* or even favor that least common denominator, the loincloth. He may play polo and be plus four at golf, or he may hunt jaguars with a spear. More typically, he may speak, in addition to his own Castilian, the French of Paris and the English of Oxford; quote Dante in the original; delight and faintly shame you with an easy erudition as unpretentious as it is profound. . . .

The Colombians are generous, proud and sensitive; they love ideas and respect those who use them, and enjoy what Lopez de Mesa calls "a spiritual agility"; they have a keen and very adult sense of humor, a tendency to chips on the shoulder, and innate and effortless courtesy, and an enviable level of culture. Their family feeling is strong, and so is their group and regional solidarity, but they are intensely independent, individual as are the French, only to a greater degree—a personally attractive trait that has its social drawbacks. They are loyal friends and hearty enemies, and in both cases express themselves with undiscriminating vigor. Much given to discussion—which they do extremely well—and incurably devoted to politics, they write elegantly and often. . . .

Montevideo, Uruguay

From *Discovering South America,* by Lewis R. Freeman, copyright ©, 1937, by Dodd, Mead and Company, Inc., reprinted by permission.

Montevideo's radiant charm is due less to its sightly location on a rising peninsula near the mouth of the river than to its never-ending parks, plazas, gardens and open spaces. Child of the pampas, the *gaucho* had to have room to breathe and fling a rope in, even when he became a rich rancher and a landed proprietor in the city. *Parques* and *Plazoletas* have been created wherever space offered, while the flower gardens around even the modest homes recall California. With a warmth and salubrity of climate similar to that of our Pacific Southwest, one is not surprised to find here most of the same fruit and flowers as in Pasadena and Santa Barbara. One's first consciousness is of the color and perfume of the banks of climbing roses, but closer inspection reveals beds of pansies, lilies and carnations, hedges of lilac and cineraria, with flaming bougainvillea, honeysuckle, heliotrope and wistaria massed over walls and houses.

Jet Flight

BY PAUL J. C. FRIEDLANDER

As a kid of tender years in upstate New York right after World War I, I can remember how the whole town used to turn out on a Sunday afternoon to a level pasture next to the city's golf course to watch the local daredevil, a flying lieutenant just back from France, put his baling wire and canvas biplane through an hour of stunt flying. This was sixteen years after the airplane had first been flown successfully by the Wright Brothers, and despite the wartime heroics of the flying aces, even children like myself, thrilled as we were, could not quite believe that *we* would live long enough to fly casually as passengers in what was then pronounced and spelled "aeroplane."

World War II so accelerated the passage of inventive time that we have managed to fly unconcernedly across most of the seven seas and six continents. Our contemporaries who might not normally qualify for membership in the Explorers Club or even as world travelers, speak nonchalantly of flying here and there, of preferences for particular planes, of happy and unhappy experiences at airports as remote as Tunis, Iceland, or Karachi.

The history of commercial aviation actually goes back only to about 1930, for the daredevils who flew as paying passengers before that were recruited principally from the rich, the glamorous, and those accustomed to tossing a long scarf (silk for females, heavier silk or wool for males) around the neck and over the port shoulder. The Tri-motor Ford and the Douglas planes, the DC-2 and the DC-3, brought the commercial passenger in out of the propeller slip stream and made flying comfortable, reasonably safe, and profitable. From fabulous speeds of 160 miles an hour in the twin-engine DC-3, we raced forward through the DC-4 and the DC-6 and the Constellation to 300 miles an hour, then to 345 in the DC-7; and now we have leaped to the next plateau, just below the speed of sound, somewhere between 550 and 600 miles an hour, with the Boeing 707 and Douglas DC-8.

As new post-war planes—piston-engine, turbo-prop and jet—joined the heavenly argosies of magic sails, I was fortunate enough to have the opportunity to sample most of them. To me and the others who sampled the jets in their earliest days, the leap into the jet age seemed less full blown and more of a comprehensive, step-by-step advancement to this new level of flying experiences. While the emphasis on the jet itself is only natural, it puts it on the means rather than the end, since passenger flying's *raison d'etre* is to carry people from one spot in the world to another. The jet does it quicker and smoother and with less effort on the part of the passenger, and these three reasons are good enough to justify its existence.

There are no serious transition problems for the experienced plane passenger. Inside the cabin the jet planes look like the piston-engine planes except that they are bigger, have more headroom, the windows perhaps a bit bigger than those of yesterday.

The difference comes in the flying, and the biggest difference is in the speed. My flight from the Pacific Ocean to the Atlantic, from Seattle to Baltimore, took only three hours and forty-eight minutes. All this country traversed in less time than it then took to fly from New York to Miami, Florida, a mere 1,100 miles, and with much less wear and tear on the passengers. Inside the cabin there is virtually no difference in sensation between the speed of piston-engine planes and the twice-as-fast jets; the ground lying far below, with no immediate orientation points to measure the speed against, unrolls slowly at 300 miles an hour, seemingly no faster at 600. You are almost twice as high in a jet, almost twice as remote.

The piston-engine plane shakes the living daylights out of everyone aboard because it is a reciprocating engine driven by thousands of gasoline explosions a minute. Anything that reciprocates mechanically is bound to shake and vibrate as it moves back and forth; add to this the explosions and you can appreciate why the silverware rattles on your airplane tray, why the floor and seat frame jiggle constantly, why the transmission of these vibrations and noises to the human body fatigues the passenger so quickly. It is the effect of the vibration and the explosive noise of the engines' exhaust that wears out plane passengers, not the physical effects of flying. The jet engine burns a steady brilliant flame, and it drives itself and the airplane forward by the reaction to the rearward thrust of its blasting jet exhaust. This is a big steady noisy whoosh, but the passenger is insulated from the noise by the fuselage and by the fact that the exhaust blasts backward, thus away from the airplane and its passengers. One can talk in normal tones without hearing the engines. The silverware doesn't rattle on the dinner tray, you can stand nickels and quarters on edge, balance spoons, pencils and cigarettes on cocktail glasses. All this means the passengers' bones and brains don't rattle, and he arrives at his destination fresh, unruffled, nerves and hair both neatly in place.

This sensation of smoothness begins as the plane starts down the runway for take-off. There is none of the burly noise and bustle of a piston-engine take-off; the jets roar a bit but the plane starts smoothly down the runway with a feeling of authority and certainty that moves up through the seats into the passenger. There is a directness about the drive of a jet down the runway that makes one feel positive that it is going to go on and up.

Landings, too, have a more positive feeling. In letting down the Boeing 707 flight from Seattle onto Baltimore, the pilot spiraled the big plane down almost vertically. And when he leveled off over the field, the big plane came in smooth and steady. You may have noticed the way the word "steady" keeps popping up. That is the best word for the way a jet performs—it flies steady, it takes off and lands steady; its steadiness removes once and for all time the rock, bump, roll and shake associated with the earlier generations of aviation.

This smoothness in flight is going to make flying much more palatable to those who found the noise and vibration wearing on the eyes, ears and other parts of the human frame. But it is the speed that makes the big difference. Four to four and a half hours across the United States, five and a half to six and a half hours between the United States and Europe, comparable 50 per cent reductions in flight time to South America and Asia and Australia—such timetables are the warp and woof for knitting the far flung continents together into one world. The traveler in a hurry will no longer spend an uneconomic part of his holiday time in travel; instead he will get where he is going in a matter of hours, stepping off his jet plane fresh, relaxed, ready, and r'arin' to go.

Taking A Picture

I would like to tell the story of the picture of the Hirosaki Castle reproduced on pages 126 and 127. Hirosaki is the name of a feudal village approximately 400 miles north of Tokyo. Every Spring at Cherry Blossom time there is a Children's festival and farmers from miles around bring their young ones to the village. I had happened to see a small black and white photograph of the castle published in Holiday magazine and wrote to my Japanese friend Tony Kawai, a photographer who usually acts as my guide, advisor and interpreter during my visits to Japan, to ask what he thought about the picture possibilities of the place. He said it would be ideal, especially at Cherry Blossom time. The exact day the blossoms are at their best varies from year to year, and they stay on the trees only two or three days. Tony told me his brother, working in Hirosaki, would make arrangements for models and keep us informed about the progress of the Cherry Blossoms. Meanwhile, Tony and I traveled about Japan photographing in Kyoto, Nara, and at the foot of Mt. Fuji. When Tony's brother let us know that the time was drawing near for the blossoms, we made our way to Hirosaki via plane, car and train and arrived at the station at 11 p.m. where we were met by Tony's brother. He took us to a little Japanese Inn, and sitting cross-legged on the huton in a room lit only from a charcoal fire in the brazier, we drank Japanese saki, a cross between scotch and rye, and talked over the plans for the next day's photographing. Good weather was forecast and the Principal of a dressmaking school was to have two of her most beautiful pupils, who were to be our models, ready at 7:30 a.m., all dressed up in their best kimonos. After a good night's sleep, Japanese fashion with the mattress laid directly on the satami, we awoke to find a hazy spring day with the sun filtering softly through the scattered clouds. Just the kind of weather to get a good picture. We picked up the girls who were to be our models accompanied by their teacher and much to my surprise they were tall, even by American standards. I was told that tall girls are not unusual for this part of the country. At the castle I chose what I thought was the best location and set up my camera. Everything was perfect; the newly painted red bridge in the foreground, a nice frame of cherry blossoms in full bloom, the angle of the sun, and the models and camera in position—but to me the setting was incomplete without a parasol. We had to send a messenger to find one, which was difficult because this far north parasols were not commonly used. During our wait for the messenger to return, crowds of local people gathered about and took pictures of me. Tony's brother had put a story in the local paper about my project and it seems that I was the first non-Japanese photographer ever to visit Hirosaki—somewhat of a curiosity. Finally, a parasol arrived and in five minutes I had the pictures finished. While I was shooting, a little Japanese man came out of the crowd and took the same scene and later won first prize with it in a Japanese photo contest.

BLACKIE KRONFELD